ENDORSEMENTS

Michael gets learning and teaching. He is in tune with the challenges teachers face in a complex environment. His strategies cut through the politics of distraction to make a difference where it really matters, which is in the classroom. This book has provided me with the tools to build teacher efficacy and better learners in the classroom. In my 10 years as a leader of pedagogy, I haven't had any other experiences that have gained more traction with students and teachers than Michael's work.

Carlo Trimboli, Leader of Pedagogy
St. Joseph's College, Banora Point, Australia

This book is a must-read for like-minded educationalists who put the child at the center of their practice. Whether you are a novice to the world of PBL or you are well seasoned with the phenomenon, this book is invaluable and will guide you through the language of learning, be it through the lens of PBL or the day-to-day practices of being a teacher.

Eoin Shinners, Principal
Limerick Educate Together Secondary School, Ireland

The Project Habit: Making Rigorous PBL Doable lays out a clear path for educators looking to enhance student engagement and deepen student learning through straightforward, actionable steps. While many educators aspire to implement high-quality, rigorous PBL, designing and implementing a unit can feel daunting. This book provides accessible strategies and examples that allow educators to shift their practice and maintain focus on what matters most, student learning.

Megan Pacheco, Executive Director
Challenge Success, Stanford, California

Shifting how we think and act to enable today's learners is no easy feat. *The Project Habit* provides just that, a shift. Deep thinking and rich action.

Gregory Tyszkiewicz, Coordinator and Primary Teacher
Our Lady Queen of Peace Primary School, Greystanes, Australia

Thought-provoking, actionable, and challenging in all the right ways, *The Project Habit* is filled with useful strategies that can be implemented immediately. Seamlessly tying together *Teaching for Transfer, Rigorous PBL by Design,* and James Clear's *Atomic Habits, The Project Habit* presents a stepwise approach to preparing for and tackling the complexities that arise before, during, and post a project. The book guides educators to consider how to get the best out of students by habit-building the critical skills required for students to experience success and demonstrate real and measurable learning in a well-planned project. This is the ultimate tool to add to a teacher's toolbox—providing real examples, usable templates, and well-designed habits that every teacher can consider implementing in their classroom.

Emmie Cossell, Secondary Science Teacher
Matthew Flinders Anglican College, Sunshine Coast, Australia

Michael McDowell's new book, *The Project Habit: Making Rigorous PBL Doable,* ought to come with a warning label: "Thinking Required." This is no recipe book for easy-to-do projects. Rather, McDowell draws on research and practice to push readers to reconsider everything from project launch to final reflection. ("Question everything" is #9 on McDowell's list of teaching habits worth cultivating.) His end goal—deeper, more equitable learning—makes this a challenge worth taking.

Suzie Boss, PBL advocate and author *of Project Based Teaching: How to Create Rigorous and Engaging Learning Experiences*

McDowell and Miller's *The Project Habit* successfully bridges the gap between adopting the pedagogical approaches that most impact student learning and . . . making instructional change manageable and sustainable for teachers. McDowell and Miller support educators in moving from motion into action while ensuring their focus remains on building strong learning cultures and enabling students to demonstrate their understanding at the surface, deep, and transfer levels of learning complexity. Providing rich examples, scaffolds, protocols, and templates, *The Project Habit* will provide teachers and leaders with the support they need to put into action the approaches that work best in learning, whether in the context of project-based learning or the mainstream classroom.

Kurt Challinor, Lead, Secondary Learning and Teaching
Catholic Schools Office, Diocese of Lismore, Australia

McDowell and Miller provide a practical, common sense approach to student learning through the lens of project based learning. More importantly, they offer a guide to closing the feedback loop with students, a task that can feel daunting at the best of times. Student engagement and achievement soared in my class when I applied the time saving strategies outlined in The Project Habit. This is a must read for any teacher that wants to engage, teach and refine student learning.

Stephanie Trott, Social Studies Teacher
Redwood Middle School, Napa, California

THE
PROJECT
HABIT

Making
Rigorous PBL
Doable

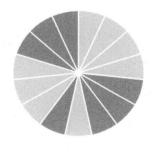

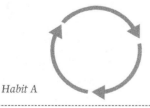

Habit A

Michael
McDowell

Habit B

Kelley S.
Miller

Foreword by Guy **Claxton**

For information about this title or to order other books and/or electronic media, contact the publisher:

Mimi and Todd Press
4629 Cass St. #292
San Diego, CA 92109
www.mimitoddpress.com

ISBN: 978-1-950089-12-3 (paperback)
          978-1-950089-13-0 (ebook)

Printed in the United States of America

Program Director: Paul J. Bloomberg, Ed.D.
Publishing Manager: Tony Francoeur
Production Coordinator: Lisa Cebelak
Copy Editor: Terri Lee Paulsen
Line Editor: Rita Carlberg
Book Designer/Typesetter: Van-Garde Imagery, Inc.
Indexer: Maria Sosnowski
Cover Designer: Alison Cox
Creative Director and Graphic Design: Alison Cox
Marketing Manager: Jace McCracken
Office Manager: Leah Tierney

Online resources are available at mimitoddpress.com/the-project-habit

ACKNOWLEDGMENTS

While learning is often done in the company of others, writing is a solitary task. My immense gratitude goes to the village that surrounded my family so that I was never truly working alone. The invisible labor of car pools, pizza dinners, and extended playdates is what gave me the time it took to co-author this book. Thank you to the Ex family, Southam family, Chatham family, Martha Clements, and the dear friends in my community who share the joy and labor of child-rearing with me. Much appreciation for the teachers and fellow learners in Napa Valley and beyond who continue to shape a more innovative and equitable vision for education; we learn something from each other daily. Unending thanks to my husband and my parents, lifelong learners who wondered why I hadn't written a book already. And tremendous gratitude to Michael, who made sure we remedied that problem.

Kelley S. Miller

In 2017, when the book *Rigorous PBL by Design* was published, a great number of teachers, leaders, parents, and students embarked on a new journey of learning. This learning occurred around the world in every context imaginable, and I was overwhelmed by the impact, innovation, imagination, and inquiry that ensued.

In addition, I was blessed with feedback on how we could go further in our teaching, leading, and learning. I'm indebted to those educators, students, and families for sharing their journey with me in how to improve the learning lives of children. This book is for them and the new learnings we have codified from the original text. Kelley S. Miller is one of those trailblazers. I'm grateful to her for her experience, clarity in writing, expertise in teaching and leading, and passion for pursuing what's next in education.

Thank you to Lisa, Alison, Paul, and Tony at Mimi & Todd Press and The Core Collaborative for your grace, clarity, support, and drive. As always, to Quinn, Harper, and Asher. I love you and thank you for your patience and grace.

Michael McDowell, Ed.D.

CONTENTS

Chapter 1

Rigorous PBL: Overview 1

Chapter 2

Rigorous PBL: Planning

	Habit 4: **Lock it (the schedule) in** by setting tentative dates for workshops aligned to complexity levels	58

	Conclusion	63
	Review Questions	64
	Next Steps	65

Phase 1: Project Launch 67

	Habit 5: **Start with a challenge** by setting your purpose with an entry event and getting students clear on what they're learning and what success looks like	69

	Habit 6: **Name the gaps** by pre-assessing and discussing the results with students	86

Chapter 4

Phase 2: Building Knowledge 111

Chapter 5

Phase 3: Deep-Learning Workshops 127

	Habit 9: Question everything together through structured discussions, deep-level feedback strategies, and formative assessments	132

	Conclusion	153
	Review Questions	153
	Next Steps	154

Chapter 7

Inspecting Our Impact

 Online Appendix — mimitoddpress.com/the-project-habit

FOREWORD

Any method of teaching can be done well or badly. Didactic instruction can be extreme—mind-numbingly dull and formulaic—or it can be fascinating and enlightening. Project-based Learning (PBL) can be ill judged—creating confusion, frustration, and stagnation—or it can stretch, strengthen, and deepen students' knowledge, intellectual expertise, and indeed their sophistication as independent learners. Teaching well is a matter of judgment, continually reviewed and adapted in response to its effects. Its success depends on sensitivity to the mood of a class, to students' existing knowledge, their degree of interest in the topic, the intrinsic difficulties and demands of the topic itself, and the familiarity and comfortableness of both teachers and their students with that method of teaching.

PBL has been the subject of much polemical and polarized hostility from some teachers and educators. They have seen it done badly, or have tried it out themselves with high hopes, and it has not gone well, and they have leaped to the conclusion that the entire methodology is misconceived, or even downright damaging (especially to already disadvantaged students). But such knee-jerk condemnation is premature. First, they should have wondered: Hmm, perhaps this PBL business is more subtle and demanding than I thought. Perhaps the students didn't have the sufficient background knowledge to make sense of the challenge I gave them; perhaps I needed to have taught them more before I introduced the project. Or maybe I overestimated the degree of responsibility or complexity that that group of students were able to handle. Perhaps they were so conditioned to being told what to do that they were simply thrown, made anxious or suspicious, by being asked to think for themselves. Perhaps students' capacity for self-management and collaboration has to be seen developmentally, as reflecting skills and attitudes that need a slowly escalating diet of challenge and skillfully targeted coaching if they are to grow successfully over time. Maybe I should be more cautious next time or choose a more amenable class in which to try out something new. Maybe I have a lot to learn if I am going to do PBL well. Indeed, PBL may have been 'oversold' to such teachers by enthusiastic authors and consultants who set them up with naive expectations that were bound to be disappointing and have resulted in disillusionment and cynicism.

It is true that simplistic and exaggerated claims have been made by both "traditionalists" and "progressives," but we should move quickly on from such slanging matches to more fruitful discussions of appropriateness, moderation, and balance. The issue is not which approach to adopt ideologically but when, with whom, for what purposes, and in what combinations different elements of the teachers' tool kit are best deployed. Teachers' *explanations*, students' *explorations*, and teacher, peer, or self-*evaluations* all have their place and should be blended and varied judiciously. But such flexible and contingent teaching is demanding and sophisticated, and many teachers, if they are to master it, will have to tinker gently and persistently with their own engrained habits. And they will need helpful scaffolding and coaching to do it. And that is exactly what Michael McDowell and Kelley S. Miller set out to provide in this timely and important new book.

It may or may not be true, as the old proverb has it, that the road to hell is paved with good intentions—but the road to educational stagnation certainly is. As McDowell and Miller point out, the educational wrecker yards around the world are full of the rusting remains of once shiny new plans for educational reform. One reason for this wastage is the volatility of the political weather, as incoming administrations make a habit of overriding decent innovations that do not fit their simplistic ideologies. But another is the persistent failure of reforms to factor in and counteract the strong inertia of teachers' classroom habits, and the school structures and cultures within which teachers have to operate. McDowell and Miller make the point with a nice quote from James Clear, the author of the best-selling *Atomic Habits*. "You do not rise to the level of your goals. You fall to the level of your systems. Your goal is your desired outcome. Your system is the collection of daily habits that will get you there [or not!].

This year, spend less time focusing on outcomes and more time focusing on the habits that precede the results." If today's well-planned educational reforms are to become tomorrow's new normal, then the planning has to include detailed, subtle, realistic advice about how existing habits are to be systematically transmuted into embedded changes in classroom cultures—and hardheaded ideas about how these habits change methods are to be resourced, disseminated, and quality assured.

For this realignment to happen, teachers will need time and ongoing professional development, and *The Project Habit* provides a vital manual for teachers and their coaches. Well-referenced and firmly grounded in current research, this book—coupled, perhaps, with Dylan Wiliam's equally valuable ideas about how to design and run professional learning communities in schools—should make an ideal collaborative workbook to guide busy teachers' efforts to tweak their teaching styles so that elements of project-based learning become not occasional frenzies of enthusiastic but unfocused experimentation but infused, embedded strands of the learning-centered cultures they intentionally create in their classrooms. Education has urgently to lift its gaze from the habitual obsession with teachable knowledge and high-stakes examinations and better prepare students—in Art Costa's neat phrase—not (just) for a life of tests but for the tests of life. And if it is to do that, rigorous, well-designed, continuous PBL has to become the norm.

Guy Claxton

Author of *The Learning Power Approach: Teaching Learners to Teach Themselves* (Corwin, 2018) and *The Future of Teaching and the Myths That Hold It Back* (Routledge, 2021)

INTRODUCTION

> " Motion will never produce a final result. Action will.
>
> —James Clear

Struggling farmer Ray Kinsella moves slowly through a sea of cornstalks. The waning Iowa daylight turns to dusk as his shoulders brush row after row of corn. Behind Ray, his wife and daughter sit on the porch swing. The setting is bucolic, but times are hard. He doesn't know how he'll make ends meet. A quiet wind rustles across the corn tassels. And then Ray hears one of the most iconic lines in movie history: "If you build it, he will come." *Field of Dreams* is born: inspired by an otherworldly voice, Ray builds a baseball field among the corn rows to fulfill his dreams and save the family farm.

This story sounds great. If we only build the things we need, then results will happen. If only we have the right meal plan, we'll sleep better at night. If we research the right exercise strategy, we'll surely lose weight. As teachers, if we meticulously develop the perfect unit plan, then students will emerge as better writers, collaborators, and thinkers. We are certainly willing to put in the work of preparation; we trust that if we prepare well, we will reap the benefits of the work that is truly required. We may read a book on meal planning, meet with a trainer to discuss exercise routines, or spend days in professional learning to hone our unit planning process. Those activities are helpful. However, they shouldn't be confused with results.

Planning, strategizing, and learning are motions we go through so that action can take shape. They are an important process of building and planning, but they are not the same as the daily actions it takes to meet goals. It is the action in the moment that produces the results we aim for. Action, at the time that it's needed, will deliver an outcome. Action is choosing salad even when you're in a rush. It's doing three sets of crunches every other day even if there's family in town. Action is seeking feedback from students, even if it means you'll need to do tomorrow differently.

When I (Michael) was a child in rural Oklahoma, my neighbor used to use the adage "mowing the lawn without turning on the mower" when someone went through the motions of labor but didn't do the actual work. Motion work is cyclical—learn, plan, strategize, repeat. Make no mistake, work is being done in this process, but it is not a substitute for taking the action necessary to improve results. You're mowing the lawn without turning on the mower. Action is linear. Action is about doing the work; it's turning on the mower and cutting the grass. Results happen here.

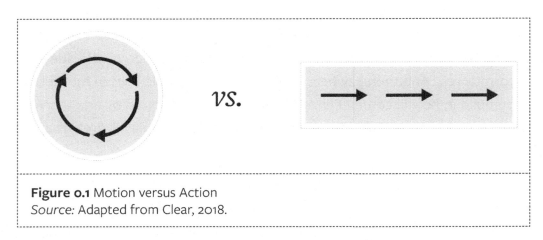

Figure 0.1 Motion versus Action
Source: Adapted from Clear, 2018.

We love to feel like we are making progress, and we hate to fail. James Clear illuminated this dichotomy well in his 2018 bestseller *Atomic Habits*. In the book, he concedes the obvious: motion habits are a necessary part of planning; we have to start somewhere. But we get stuck in between our best plans and our most tangible actions. Often, the culprit for planning but not doing is our desire for a sense of safety. When we plan, we enjoy the intuitive feeling that we are making progress without risking failure. As Clear (2018) shared in a subsequent blog, "Most of us are experts at avoiding criticism. It doesn't feel good to fail or to be judged publicly, so we tend to avoid situations where that might happen. And that's the biggest reason why you slip into motion rather than taking action: you want to delay failure." One place we are quick to avoid that risk is the classroom. (see Table 0.1)

Out-of-School Fears That Keep Us in the Motion Cycle	In-School Fears That Keep Us in the Motion Cycle
I'd like to get in shape. But I don't want to look stupid in the gym, so I'll buy a membership and hope that coerces me to go once in a while.	I'd like to teach using an innovative approach. But I don't want to risk confusing my students, so I'll design a unit but not quite finish it.
I'd like to land more clients for my business. But if I ask for the sale, I might get turned down. So maybe I should just email 10 potential clients instead.	I'd like to incorporate peer feedback in my lesson. But it might flop. So I'll buy another book about feedback and put it on my shelf.
I'd like to lose weight. But prepping vegetables in the morning takes too long. So maybe I'll build a meal plan that I can try out next year.	I'd like to try launching my project in a different way. But I don't want to be the weird one who does it differently. So I'll plan it and save it in my files, just in case.

Table 0.1 Fears and Motion Cycles
Source: Adapted from Clear, 2018.

Motion habits can be a deceptive mirage. It's easy to get caught up in motion habits in schools and think we're making progress. We believe we are "doing" work when, in fact, the gap between what we know and what we do widens. We think, *I've just developed a project and shared my plans with colleagues. This is good. We're doing*

PBL! Or, *I just brainstormed three or four ideas for an assessment. This is coming together.* When we plan and never get to practicing, we are in motion habit central. As James Clear (2018) shares, "Motion makes you feel like you're getting things done. But really, you're just preparing to get something done. When preparation becomes a form of procrastination, you need to change something. You don't want to merely be planning. You want to be practicing." Table 0.2 offers a few comparisons between action and motion habits in and out of the classroom.

Outside-School Examples	Within-School Examples
If I outline 20 ideas for articles I want to write, that's motion. If I write and publish an article, that's action.	If I create a project-based unit, that's motion. If I co-construct with students to develop the driving question, then I'm in action.
If I make a list of 10 potential new leads for my business, that's motion. If I reach out to one and turn her into a customer, that's action.	If I write the rubric for success, that's motion. If students actually use the success criteria to self-assess and give peers feedback, that's action.
If I read up on better diet plans, that's motion. If I eat a healthy meal, that's action.	If I search for a better project idea and read a few books on the topic, that's motion. If I implement transfer-level strategies in the class at the beginning of the unit with students, that's action.
If I go to the gym and ask about getting a personal trainer, that's motion. If I actually step under the bar and start squatting, that's action.	If I go to a conference and ask about getting coaching, that's motion. If I actually use what I learned with students, that's action.
If I study for a test or prepare for a research project, that's motion. If I take the test or write my research paper, that's action.	If I develop an assessment or review student data from an assessment, that's motion. If I use the data to change my practice or see students change their behavior based on my responses, that's action.

Table 0.2 Comparing and Contrasting Action and Motion Habits

The Design and Implementation Conundrum

Education is chock-full of books that support "motion" habits. Any book (this one included) that provides a set of planning documents, templates, and strategies to prepare for action can get more information into teachers' heads. But that is not the same as getting it into our bones and forming new habits.

Work intended to improve student clarity is a prime example of this. Schools all over the world spend a significant amount of time identifying outcomes, building sophisticated rubrics, and showcasing them on their classroom walls. Yet students often still don't understand the expectations (Nuthall, 2007). That's because designing success criteria is a motion habit. Going through the motions to write down learning intentions and success criteria is a good start, but it's no guarantee that students will be with you. The teacher who wordsmiths a perfect learning outcome and leaves it on the board is likely to still have students who are simply thinking about other things. When students aren't clear, they can't parse the difference between learning and simply completing the assignment. The context of the unit, due dates, and who gets to work with whom muddle a clear understanding of what is to be learned.

Specific interactions between teachers and students are required to ensure students are clear. After the initial "teacher work" of identifying what students need to learn, ongoing action with students is what demystifies the learning process. The moves that are most pivotal in the classroom occur when students and teachers are working together. Co-constructing success criteria by looking at examples, using success criteria to trace the path of learning, and referencing success criteria for feedback are habits that necessitate mutual action. Excellent and necessary motion work is done in the controlled, predictable space of planning alone or in teams. Action work happens in the noisy, unpredictable space of classrooms.

Feedback poses a similar conundrum. At its best, it can double the rate of learning. At its worst, it can be time intensive and produce miniscule results. The reason for this is that students require significantly different instructional and feedback strategies at different levels of learning (Hattie & Donoghue, 2016; Hattie & Timperley, 2007). As such, teachers require agile habits of assessing student performance and adapting both how they teach and how they implement feedback to where students are at that moment in time. For instance, many students need direct instruction and deliberate practice when they are first learning new material. If we fail to incorporate such tools into our classroom, then students will move forward with a gap in the foundational skills they need. As students gain proficiency, direct instruction is less effective and teachers must pivot to strategies that foster classroom discussions, evaluation and reflection, and peer-to-peer feedback (Hattie & Donoghue, 2016).

Project-based learning (PBL) is no exception to the pitfalls of planning versus doing. Books about PBL—of which there are many—revolve around building grand units of study, structuring project tasks, and forming work groups. There is a danger that this can translate into a self-fulfilling process of motion habits in the classroom. Teachers spend a lot of time planning for a great project, and students spend a lot of time making sure their product is ready for presentation night. We have motions of learning begetting more motions of learning for the sake of a project, rather than the action it takes to ensure rigorous learning is taking place in a reasonable amount of time. Moreover, PBL books often push teachers to design for wholesale changes in the design process. The message these books convey is that teachers need to over-haul everything, when perhaps a small change in a few actions is all that is needed to promote innovative learning for students. Myths pervade, including "trusting the process" and embracing the "messy middle," perpetuating beliefs that a well-designed plan will guarantee action.

This book was not written in pursuit of overhauls. In fact, most of the habits in this book will deepen learning with or without PBL. Rather than being beholden to a doctrine of projects, this text explores habits that are applicable for any classroom that puts learning at its center. Teachers and school systems that seek to begin or continue problem- and project-based learning will find that the habits within this text fit nicely into the flow of PBL instruction. Those who would rather pick one habit that piques their interest and give it a go are welcome here as well. We won't ask you to trust the process. We ask you to trust the research and trust the evidence your own students bring. And where certain actions could be made even better, we encourage teachers to diverge.

Proponents of PBL love to say students learn by doing. It is also true that students learn *better* when their teachers are doing specific things as well. "Responsive" and "agile" are better descriptors of impactful teaching than "well rehearsed" and "meticulously designed." We need to develop, implement, and inspect action-based habits to ensure rigorous learning is occurring for all students. To begin this pursuit, let's develop a common definition of rigor.

Defining Rigorous Learning

Rigorous learning may be best defined as the equal intensity and integration of surface, deep, and transfer learning within the context of a shared responsibility of learning:

* **Rigor:** Rigor is the equal intensity and integration of surface, deep, and transfer learning. A rigorous unit of study would consist of intentional instructional strategies and assessments targeted at each level of learning—surface, deep, and transfer.

* **Surface-level learning:** This is the ability for an individual to understand one or more concepts but not the ability to make connections between concepts. For example, surface-level learning is evident when students can understand basic facts and critical vocabulary terms.

* **Deep-level learning:** This is the ability for an individual to relate concepts but not the ability to apply the concepts to one or more contexts. When students can determine cause and effect or compare and contrast two different facts, they are engaged in deep-level learning.

* **Transfer-level Learning:** This is an individual's ability to appropriately apply a concept, skill, or theory within a domain of knowledge to a new context. It is the ultimate goal of education—the most applicable level of learning. Transfer-level learning is the application of knowledge and skills acquired at the surface and deep levels, and it occurs when students can apply their content knowledge and skills to multiple real-world contexts.

❋ **Shared responsibility of learning:** Students and teachers work together to ensure everyone is learning at high levels and that students are developing the knowledge and skills to become their own teachers.

Habits that are linked to rigorous learning enable students to develop the following outcomes:

❋ **Confidence** – the ability to handle ambiguity and setbacks, work with others, and develop assessment capabilities as a learner

❋ **Competence** – the development of knowledge and skills across surface, deep, and transfer levels of complexity

As such, we need teaching habits that provide students with strategies at the level of complexity they are facing, along with strategies that build a shared responsibility of learning. This definition requires habits that adjust to the level of learning that students need.

As we will see throughout the book, implementing these habits takes time, energy, and often the effort to buck the trends of the past in PBL work and in the traditional educational space. The research is very clear that PBL has a minimal impact on student learning unless specific habits are in place (Hattie, 2009). However, recent studies show that when specific habits are embedded in the classroom, the yield for student learning is substantial (Krajcik et al. 2021). Unfortunately, the actual classroom practices in both PBL and traditional classrooms that are required to build student competence and confidence continue to be the exception rather than the rule.

The Case for Actionable Habits to Ensure Rigorous Learning

In March 2021, Professor Emeritus John Hattie presented at the World Education Summit and shared the following key findings:

❋ "We've just looked at 17,000 transcripts of teachers teaching classes. And two things became very clear: we could not find, across those 17,000 classrooms, a single occasion when the teacher taught a strategy of learning, nor did we see any teaching of transfer."

✳ 80% of what we teach, students already know.

✳ 70% of the questions we ask require only three words to answer.

✳ 90% of the talking in the classroom is the teacher.

✳ 80% of the feedback students give each other is incorrect.

✳ "When you ask them [students], 'Who's the best learner in the class?' They say, 'Person X because she knows lots, and she doesn't need to put any effort to knowing lots'—the antithesis of good learning."

Think about your own school, classroom, or system. Do those statistics strike a familiar tone to what is happening in your classrooms? If so, you're not alone. Studies have demonstrated that teachers in U.S. schools begin with rigorous tasks but then use habits of surface learning to relieve students who are struggling. In other words, they used innovative *motion* habits to design rigorous tasks but then fell back on previous *action* habits to break the task down to make it easier for students.

Is there any doubt on the type of learning we privilege? Think of the schools or systems we teach within:

✳ Is complexity considered an event (e.g., conducting a project, going on a field trip, working with an outside agency, creating a portfolio of different work samples), or a routine practice?

✳ Are our students completing assignments that simply require regurgitating facts? Do they rely on cutting, pasting, and scrolling?

✳ Do discussions in class involve more than one point of view and require more than three words to answer?

✳ Are students involved in the feedback process?

Why do we privilege surface-level learning? Surface learning, or knowing facts and procedures, is interwoven into our pedagogy, our assessment scheme, the tasks we provide to students, and our cultural expectations. For instance, worksheets are a sign of consistency in the classroom and a symbol to parents at home that learning, regardless of quality, is happening in the school. Could you imagine a world without worksheets? Could we instead imagine a world where we ensure students have the knowledge and skills to actualize their empowerment?

Empowerment

Competency is currency. When students know core content knowledge and how to apply that knowledge to diverse contexts, they will reap the benefits of being competent learners throughout adulthood. However, schools tend to fall short in giving students the opportunity to apply what they learn to new situations. One could argue that the system is built that way: teachers receive surface-level instruction in their credential programs; it is reinforced in student teaching and is what is incentivized within school evaluation systems. Even Hattie's (2009) landmark Visible Learning research found that 90% of student assessments were at the surface level. As such, habits set in. They become tacit and automatic. We continue to reinforce, and even refine, our own practices by getting better at surface teaching and learning. We do so at the expense of growing competent, empowered learners.

There is another more pernicious reason surface-level work remains persistent, and it relates to the concept of control. The need to control situations or people stems from our natural biases as humans and is sustained—overtly or subtly—in systems of oppression. These systems play out in dynamics of control in the classroom. In Haberman's (1991) writing of *Pedagogy of Poverty*, he argues that teaching and learning look like the following:

❋ Teaching is what teachers do. Learning is what students do. Therefore, students and teachers are engaged in different activities.

✳ Teachers are in charge and responsible. Students are those who still need to develop appropriate behavior. Therefore, when students follow teachers' directions, appropriate behavior is being taught and learned.

Even high-impact strategies are largely grafted to meet the needs of control. Take, for instance, the substantial effect of clarity on student achievement. Students are directed to recite standards on the board rather than co-construct with peers and teachers. Classroom discourse is often denatured to repeat surface-level knowledge. Control is baked into the DNA of many classrooms.

We describe control as *giving up* control to a person or a situation or *taking* control of a person or a situation. When engaged in incorrectly, pedagogies such as problem-based learning often give up control to students and leave them without the knowledge, skills, and support they need to be successful. Conversely, didactic instruction can become about student compliance. These are two sides of the same coin. Each assumes that one person or group inherently holds the power, which they are entitled to or relinquish. In perceiving control as transactional, we uphold an educational system that is akin to banking: input, output, give, and take. We miss the greater potential of what Paulo Freire (2000) calls dialogue in problem-posing education: "The teacher is no longer merely the-one-who-teaches, but one who is himself taught in dialogue with the students, who in turn while being taught also teach. They become jointly responsible for a process in which all grow" (p. 80).

The opposite of overvaluing surface learning can also be true. Teachers may scrap surface learning and slide their chips across the table to transfer-level learning. Student-centered mantras fill school halls and demand a shift in the power dynamic from teacher centered to student controlled. When the pendulum swings to the far side of rigor, we witness unguided inquiry. Products and projects hold a prized status over evidence of foundational learning, and emotional engagement is sacrosanct. The problem is, a heart without a mind leaves students unprepared for the future of learning, living, and making a positive impact on others. Swinging to the other side of the rigor-and-responsibility pendulum may have the appearance of empowerment, but the results can be dismal. By removing a means for foundational learning, those who we intend to empower, we can mistakenly impoverish.

Equity

When students enter our classrooms with significant gaps in their learning, the stakes are too high to use an instructional model that may leave them even farther behind. As such, critics of contemporary models of project-based learning have good reason to sound alarm bells. The largest-scale meta-analysis, conducted by professor John Hattie, illustrated that PBL has a marginal positive impact on student learning (Hattie, 2009). Kirschner et al. (2006) illustrate that without intentional guidance during a PBL unit, students will fail to learn surface and deep knowledge. On the other hand, if PBL is a model that "only works for students who are ready," it practically ensures that those with fewer resources at home will remain starved of meaningful ways to apply what they learn. When adults position students to stay in a perpetual cycle of surface learning, we become the gatekeepers of rich and robust experiences in school.

Rigorous PBL is meant to promote surface, deep, and transfer learning for all students. It places equal emphasis on the need to build fluency, engage in critical thinking through dialogue, and create solutions to nuanced problems. It takes seriously the idea that rigor requires each level and all students are capable of accessing and reaching such levels. Moreover, when we take it upon ourselves to ensure students are clear on what they are learning and advocate for their next steps, we are enacting an expectation that every student should have a voice in their learning.

Developing assessment capabilities, ensuring accurate peer-to-peer feedback, and handling ambiguity in a supportive and social context are components of equity. These approaches empower learners to engage successfully not only independently but interdependently. They assume that the whole student, regardless of prior achievement or background, is an asset to their own learning and also an important contributor to the group's learning as a whole. From this standpoint, PBL is no longer a risky choice—instead, rigorous PBL is an informed instructional decision to accelerate the learning of all students.

Engagement

We cannot discuss empowerment and equity without bringing up one of the most tangible ways they manifest in classrooms: student engagement. Consider the seventh graders who choose to sit in the back row, bodies slumped and minds on literally anything else. Consider students in their first years of elementary school, full of energy and imagination at recess but decidedly distracted when it comes to reading. How do we bring them in? To say it is simply a matter of letting students choose what they learn overlooks the fact that we do, in fact, have certain standards to teach. As a result, the way we talk about engagement is often closely related to issues of control. Consider the predominant assumptions about direct instruction and project-based learning. Direct instruction has connotations of rigidity and passive, obedient students. PBL implies infinite student choice and controlled chaos. How do both methodologies address the following questions:

❋ How do we enable students to persist?

❋ What motivates students?

❋ How do we ensure students learn at high levels?

Jim Knight (2022) explains that there are three types of engagement—behavioral, emotional, and cognitive. *Behavioral engagement* requires following directions, staying on task, and adhering to classroom norms. Behavioral engagement asks: Are students on task? Are students participating? To be behaviorally engaged is to follow directions, reduce transition time between activities, and work quietly when asked to do so.

Emotional engagement is anchored to students' feelings of belonging, interest in the activity or task, and belief they can succeed. Key questions associated with emotional engagement include: Do students feel like they belong? Feel safe? Engage in positive and meaningful experiences at school? Do students have hope? Do they have opportunities to succeed on a daily basis? Are we tapping into their present interests? When students are emotionally engaged, they feel comfortable talking with classmates and feel safe asking for help when they need it.

Finally, *cognitive engagement* is associated with student concentration on the expected learning, progress toward learning intended outcomes, and student evaluation and reflection on their progress toward outcomes. Key questions associated with cognitive engagement include: Are students learning the intended outcomes from the activity or experience? Are we tapping into their background knowledge (even if they lack background knowledge of the content)? Cognitively engaged students have a clear understanding of their progress and leverage the thrill of marked improvement to focus their attention.

Classroom environments that privilege surface learning and the predominant methodologies (such as direct instruction) also privilege behavioral engagement. Many iterations of project-based learning privilege emotional engagement. Both approaches are rooted in beliefs about how to best move learning forward. Most surface-level strategies place teachers in the "I do" position, controlling the environment yet hoping students will take full responsibility for learning. Often in PBL, teachers take the "you do" position with very little structure and still expect students to take full responsibility for their learning. Balancing the equally crucial roles of teachers and students, along with a shared responsibility of learning, is no small task. Rigorous PBL aims to incorporate all three types of engagement by co-creating learning with the "we do" of students and teachers working together.

We need to engage in habits that leverage student empowerment, are anchored to the tenets of equity, and engage all learners. It requires a methodology that builds students' competence and confidence to face challenges, work with others, and share control over their own learning every day. This is where rigorous PBL frames the habits that are critical for teachers and students.

The Project Habit

This book centers on habits that, when routinely used, have a high probability of developing rigorous learning outcomes for students (see Figure 0.2). Eight of the habits discussed are action habits, which make up the heart of this book. They are central to moving student learning forward and can be used by teachers who are going to engage in the entire PBL process or a teacher who wants to bring transfer to life in their current units. In other words, these habits are for everyone.

These action habits are nested between motion habits: planning and inspecting. The habits of motion are critical to preparing for, and investigating, our impact on student learning. They are meant to maximize the efficacy of those action habits we make routine in our classrooms and to help us rethink the moments that require deliberate deviations from our habits.

THE PROJECT HABIT
Making Rigorous PBL by Design Doable

Rigorous PBL Design Habit	Success Criteria
Habit 1: Make it clear	Create student-friendly learning intentions and success criteria at surface, deep, and transfer levels of learning.
Habit 2: See it everywhere	Generate multiple contexts and one or more driving questions.
Habit 3: Plan for the right fit	Align tasks across surface, deep, and transfer expectations. Design entry events, curveballs, and sequels for transfer.
Habit 4: Lock it in	Set tentative dates for workshops aligned to complexity levels.

Rigorous PBL Action Habit	Success Criteria
PHASE 1	
Habit 5: Start with a challenge *Where are we going?*	Set your purpose with an entry event. Get students clear on what they're learning and what success looks like.
Habit 6: Name the gaps *Where are we now?*	Pre-assess and discuss the results with students.
Habit 7: Look ahead *What's next?*	Create next steps based on knows/need-to-knows. Hold to learning agreements and protocols.
PHASE 2	
Habit 8: Build the foundation	Apply instructional and feedback strategies to support surface-level learning.

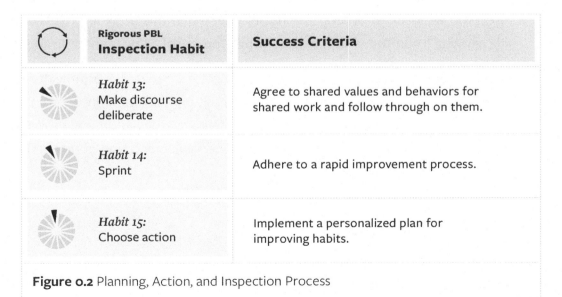

Rigorous PBL **Action Habit, cont.**	**Success Criteria**
PHASE 3	
Habit 9: Question everything together	Engage in structured discussions. Use deep-level feedback strategies. Incorporate formative assessments.
PHASE 4	
Habit 10: Return to transfer	Revisit the entry experience, driving questions, learning intentions, and success criteria to determine key knows/need-to-knows. Implement transfer-level workshops to apply learning in real-world contexts and address curveballs.
Habit 11: Deliver on the challenge	Structure means for showcasing work and giving/receiving feedback. Engage students in project sequels.
Habit 12: Look in the mirror	Conduct reflective protocols on academic growth, meeting cultural expectations, and addressing the driving question.

Rigorous PBL **Inspection Habit**	**Success Criteria**
Habit 13: Make discourse deliberate	Agree to shared values and behaviors for shared work and follow through on them.
Habit 14: Sprint	Adhere to a rapid improvement process.
Habit 15: Choose action	Implement a personalized plan for improving habits.

Figure 0.2 Planning, Action, and Inspection Process

Setting the Stage for Habits of Practice

Assuredly, a wide variety of habits could have been selected for this text. But it was important to us to be selective. After all, the point is to get to the doing of the thing rather than reading endless chapters. The following three criteria derived from Reeves (2011) were used as a filter for the selection of the 15 habits discussed in this book:

✳ **Impact:** A habit worth doing has potential to make a significant difference in student learning. We're not going for a little; we're going for a lot. As Reeves (2011) shares, "Because 95% of interventions result in some gain in achievement . . . the criterion for 'impact' must be more than 'better than nothing.' It must surpass a benchmark of real-world change" (p. 2). The habits selected here are focused on making a substantial impact on student learning.

✳ **Leverage:** A habit worth doing improves a number of student outcomes. Teachers are busy; we need to get the most out of our efforts. For instance, focusing on students co-constructing the learning intentions, success criteria, and driving questions using multiple contexts during Phase 1 enables students to gain clarity of learning, develop assessment capability, and experience deep- and transfer-level learning while gaining the foundational skills to give and receive feedback to others. The habits selected in this book are focused on leveraging a number of outcomes through the use of a few teacher strategies.

✳ **Implementation:** A habit worth doing can get even better over time. It must follow a continuum of development, mastery, and iteration. In Chapter 7, a continuum of ignition, deliberate practice, deliberate deviation, and deliberate monitoring is shown to outline the degree of implementation of high-impact practices in innovative spaces.

How This Book Is Set Up

This book has seven chapters designed to make the case for the following theory of action and meeting the following four success criteria:

Theory of Action	Success Criteria
If we develop and sustain the routine habits embedded within the Rigorous PBL by Design process, then students will develop the knowledge and skills to thrive in school, their community, and their future.	1. Understand the rationale for planning, taking action, and inspecting my (our) impact on student learning using Rigorous PBL by Design 2. Develop motion habits to design Rigorous PBL by Design units of study 3. Develop action habits to implement Rigorous PBL by Design practices 4. Develop motion habits to inspect the impact of my actions on student learning and plan for improvement and/or innovation

Table 0.3 The Project Habit: Theory of Action and Success Criteria

An outline for each chapter is described below:

Chapter 1

Chapter 1 is designed to meet success criteria 1, educator's understanding the rationale for planning, taking action, and inspecting their impact on student learning using Rigorous PBL by Design. The chapter outlines why we need to engage in rigorous teaching and learning and highlights the importance of implementing the project habits in this book.

Chapter 2

Chapter 2 is designed to meet success criteria 2, wherein practitioners develop motion habits to design Rigorous PBL by Design units of study. This chapter walks us through the motion-based habits of planning, learning, and strategizing early on in the rigorous PBL process. This chapter is lean, offering a few suggestions to get going into the action portion of the book. The online Appendix has several resources to support you during this phase. But don't stay here too long. While it feels good and gives the illusion of progress, these habits don't do much for students until the work takes place in the classroom.

Chapter 3

Chapter 3 walks us through specific actions teachers should take to engage in Phase 1 of implementing Rigorous PBL by Design. During this phase, students engage in transfer-level thinking and doing and generate strategies to problem-solve in challenging situations. Teachers simultaneously practice habits that support students in developing clarity of expectations, tracking their own progress, planning for next steps in their own learning, and giving and receiving feedback.

Chapter 4

Chapter 4 covers Phase 2 of a project and focuses on doable habits that support students in learning new content. This chapter focuses on habits that enhance direct instruction, connect learning to deeper learning and project expectations, and how to effectively enact corrective feedback strategies.

Chapter 5

Chapter 5 explains the third phase of a project and focuses on doable habits that support students in deepening their learning. It focuses on habits that center on classroom discussions, evaluation and reflection, how to connect learning to transfer learning and project expectations, and how to effectively engage in seeking help from peers and using feedback strategies aligned to complex levels of learning.

Chapter 6

Chapter 6 discusses the final phase of a project and outlines how we support students in transferring their learning. It explores habits that enhance students' abilities to evaluate across contexts, work with others in problem-solving situations, engage in changing circumstances, and present tentative solutions and reflect on performance.

Chapter 7

Chapter 7 is designed to meet success criteria 4, wherein practitioners develop motion habits to inspect the impact of their actions. This chapter outlines how we develop and sustain project habits using student data, evaluating the systems we have in place to ignite, deepen, deviate, and sustain habits for impact. Strategies are also suggested for supporting the implementation of action-based habits with fellow teachers, professional learning communities (PLCs), and school systems.

Key Lessons or Takeaways

We believe that after you read this book, the following six key lessons or takeaways will emerge for you and your team.

Key Lessons	
1.	**Rigorous PBL** centers on a set of actionable habits that ensure students have clarity of expectations, encounter and address challenging work, and are actively involved in a culture focused on growth in learning and supporting one another.
2.	**Applying project habits** is much more important than designing for project habits.
3.	**Clarity** is gained through habits of conversation, not simply presentation.
4.	Addressing **challenging** problems requires teachers and students to be flexible in which habits they use to be successful.
5.	A learning-centered **culture** requires habits that promote desirable difficulties, feedback, and diverse points of view.
6.	Teachers use evidence of teaching and learning with colleagues to improve, maintain, and deviate from practices in order to **sustain** high **impact** and high **innovation**.

THE PROJECT HABITS

 Design Habits

Habit 1
Make it clear by ensuring student-friendly learning intentions and success criteria at surface, deep, and transfer levels of learning.

Habit 2
See it (the learning) everywhere by generating multiple contexts and one or more driving questions.

Habit 3
Plan for the right fit by aligning tasks across surface, deep, and transfer expectations and designing entry events, curveballs, and sequels for transfer.

Habit 4
Lock it (the schedule) in by setting tentative dates for workshops aligned to complexity levels.

 Action Habits

Habit 5
Start with a challenge by setting your purpose with an entry event and getting students clear on what they're learning and what success looks like.

Habit 6
Name the gaps by pre-assessing and discussing the results with students.

Habit 7
Look ahead by creating next steps based on knows/need-to-knows and holding to learning agreements and protocols.

Action Habits, continued

 Habit 8
Build the foundation by applying instructional and feedback strategies to support surface-level learning.

 Habit 9
Question everything together through structured discussions, deep-level feedback strategies, and formative assessments.

 Habit 10
Return to transfer by implementing transfer-level workshops to apply learning in real-world contexts and address curveballs.

 Habit 11
Deliver on the challenge by structuring means for showcasing work and giving/receiving feedback and engaging students in project sequels.

 Habit 12
Look in the mirror by conducting reflecting protocols on academic growth, meeting cultural expectations, and addressing the driving question.

 Inspection Habits

 Habit 13
Make discourse deliberate by agreeing to shared values and behaviors for shared work and following through on them.

 Habit 14
Sprint by adhering to a rapid improvement process.

 Habit 15
Choose action by implementing a personalized plan for improving habits.

Table 0.4 The Project Habits Overview

💡 Conclusion

After reading this book, teachers will see the critical importance of focusing less on project design and more on the implementation of consistent and sustainable teaching habits. Moreover, at the end of this book, teachers will see that emphasizing small shifts in practice will enable actual changes in the classroom, greater levels of impact on students, and new innovations. Ultimately, this aims to promote a greater level of contemporary learning.

Chapter 1

RIGOROUS PBL: OVERVIEW

> " ...the purpose of learning isn't to affirm our beliefs, its to evolve our beliefs.
>
> —Adam Grant 2021

In 1949, the Mann Gulch fire was raging in the mountains of Montana. Smoke jumpers were called in to take care of the job. This was considered a routine fire, until it wasn't. As they were extinguishing the fire, the blaze changed course and rushed toward the firefighters. Although the foreman yelled for his men to drop their tools and run, only 2 of the 15 firefighters dropped their tools. The other firefighters kept their heavy gear, despite the added bulk. They perished in the fire, weighed down by their equipment and unable to climb the steep terrain. As Epstein (2019) writes, "One firefighter stopped fleeing and sat down, exhausted, never having removed his heavy pack" (p. 246).

This was an unlikely occurrence, right? While this may seem like an isolated incident, between 1990 and 1995 alone, a total of 23 wildland firefighters lost their lives trying to outrace fires uphill, even though dropping their heavy equipment could have made the difference between life and death.

Why did the firefighters not drop their tools and run? Reflecting on the Mann Gulch account, originally detailed in Norman Maclean's (1992) *Young Men and Fire*, psychologist Karl Weick shares that dropping one's tools creates an existential crisis. Without my tools, who am I?" (Grant, 2021, p. 7). He further writes, "Dropping one's tools is a proxy for unlearning, for adaptation, for flexibility. . . . It is the very unwillingness of people to drop their tools that turns some of these dramas into tragedies" (Epstein, 2019, p. 246).

Why do teachers, when faced with the opportunity to bring forward real-world problems, stick to surface-level teaching and learning? Adam Grant (2021) presents the following reasons for this error in human judgment, which the authors have adapted for the classroom (see Figure 1.1):

❋ **Assumptions:** Questioning ourselves makes the world more unpredictable. It requires us to admit that the facts may have changed, that what was once right may now be wrong. Humans of all kinds, including educators, prefer the ease of hanging on to old views and old habits over the difficulty of grappling with new ideas and practices. Therefore, we stick to our current mental models or assumptions. The firefighters struggled to question their own mental model about their identity. Firefighters do their jobs with tools distinctive to their trade; they think, *The axe is part of my identity, my strength and safety—I keep this with me!* Teachers struggle to question their own mental models about teaching. We explained learning expectations with our students; why would we stop and ensure that students clearly understand what's been shared? We think, *My initial instruction is part of my identity, what I do as a good teacher. I refrain from gathering evidence that may jeopardize that belief.*

❋ **Instincts:** Under acute stress, people typically revert to their automatic and well-learned responses. Our action habits that have been built up over time take over when we are in a stressful situation, even if our rational minds know it's not in our best interest. How many times do educators, despite high-quality training and carefully developed unit plans, fall back into the familiarity of old routines? Given the myriad of daily stressors between the tardy bell and dismissal, it's no surprise we stick to what is comfortable. Likewise, in the case of firefighters, resourceful thinking was no match for repeated actions. They had been in many firefights before, and they reverted to what they knew.

❋ **Habits:** We spend time conversing about our actions and ideas rather than inspecting them, trying new ones, and building processes for rethinking. This divergence requires a healthy cognitive bias toward action. At times, we are willing to design new habits ("motion") but neglect to engage in the new habit when it matters most. Without training and practice in new situations, firefighters don't see a need to change practice—even when a fire rages toward them. Without teachers putting habits into action, receiving support, and inspecting that work in the classroom, their practice won't change—even when an opportunity for transfer is within reach.

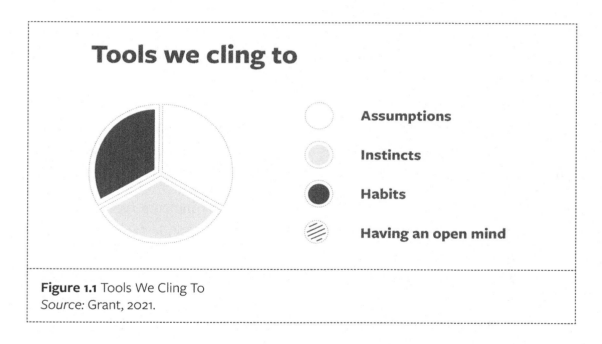

Figure 1.1 Tools We Cling To
Source: Grant, 2021.

What we can think, we can rethink. And what we learn, we can relearn. Some firefighters now train to address nonroutine situations by learning how and when to drop familiar tools and how to pick up new ones. New and complex situations may call for developing safety zones and escape fires instead of brandishing an axe or chainsaw (Rothermel, 1993). They integrated a set of tools, akin to a Swiss Army knife, to face routine and nonroutine problems.

Like firefighters, educators have a set of tools or habits—routines for teaching content, assessing student learning, and responding to student needs. If research is any predictor, deep and transfer learning is largely absent from the habits educators utilize in their daily lives. As mentioned in the introduction, 90% of teaching and learning remains at the surface level. Transfer learning is remarkably absent in classrooms, and even when highly complex tasks are introduced, they are often broken down to make them easier for students and teachers to manage.

Many of us have been trained for the predictable world of surface learning. We are familiar with direct modeling, guided practice, and independent practice to meet learning outcomes. Teachers in traditional environments have been trained to manage a classroom that resembles the inner workings of an office. Those who have been trained in project-based learning, on the other hand, have been trained to manage a classroom that resembles the inner workings of a factory floor. Perhaps a better approach would be that of an entrepreneur who is scanning the world for interconnected challenges and finding new opportunities to make the world a better place. Contemporary learning methodologies have fallen prey to the same inability to drop our tools (or habits) as traditional learning methodologies.

Moreover, we cling to designing structures and environments, rather than focus on our daily practice. Research is rife with examples. Gawande (2013) shared that since its introduction, doctors have loved anesthesia but for decades continued to struggle with daily handwashing. Hattie's (2021b) Visible Learning research shows that the factors people love and position as important in classrooms pale next to the impact of teacher expertise. However, initiatives that focus on class size, scheduling/time-tabling, and use of technology are what remain in the spotlight. "If you build it, he will come" is an implicit message that resonates in many environments.

As we will find throughout the chapter, we need to have adaptive habits that allow us to meet students where they are in their learning and to build the skills to own their learning over time. Our charge is to provide the most effective strategy at surface, deep, and transfer levels and to rethink how we engage in problem- and project-based learning. As with firefighters who have trained specifically to adapt to new situations, we must learn new tools for new situations. This requires a level of flexibility that enables us to ensure our students understand each discipline (surface and deep) and are able to move across various disciplines to solve challenging problems (transfer).

This chapter names the habits that make Rigorous PBL by Design an effective process for rethinking and relearning about our general educational practices and those of PBL in general. At the end of this chapter, you will have previewed the habits that are discussed throughout the book.

Defining Rigorous PBL

Rigorous PBL by Design is an instructional methodology that is designed to ensure all students develop confidence and competence in learning by using a problem-solving process that is thoughtfully designed and, more importantly, implemented in the classroom. RPBL is built on three key success criteria:

1. **Clarity:** Student clarity is central to a student's ability to transfer their learning, develop shared power in the classroom, and become an assessment-capable learner and to support others in doing the same. Units of study are built and daily habits are implemented to ensure students and teachers have clarity of expectations of learning, problems that they are working to solve, and means for working through both relational and problem-solving situations.

2. **Challenge:** Student and teacher habits must be aligned to the teaching and learning strategies that have the highest probability of substantially enhancing learning at the surface, deep, and transfer levels of complexity. Ensuring challenge is central to a rigorous program whereby students experience high-quality instruction, feedback, and learning strategies that are aligned to each level of learning. While all three levels of learning are critical, deep and transfer learning are critical to ignite engagement,

consolidate learning, form general principles, and use critical thinking and collaboration.

3. **Culture:** Students and teachers develop a partnership toward the continued development of dignity, belonging, and collective growth. They examine the impact of student and teacher learning. A learning-based culture is centered on the importance of promoting interdependence between students and teachers in their work to improve learning, solve problems, and develop empathy, compassion, and kindness.

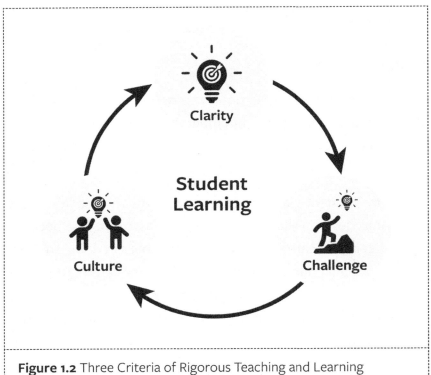

Figure 1.2 Three Criteria of Rigorous Teaching and Learning

A Solid Research Basis for Rigorous PBL by Design

RPBL grew out of a preponderance of research on student learning. This methodology is based on the work from John Hattie's synthesis of meta-analyses and continued work on the relative impact of strategies on student learning (Hattie, 2021b).

It also stands on the shoulders of other researchers and practitioners, including Robert Marzano, Dylan Wiliam, and Guy Claxton. Figure 1.3, now a familiar image in educational literature, represents a range of impacts on student learning. Hattie illustrated that almost every strategy in education improves student learning; however, some strategies have an impact that yields substantial growth for students. As such, we need to look at the magnitude or effect of strategies when we select what we will spend our time using in the classroom. In his work, he used an effect size (ES) to calculate the amount or magnitude of impact a strategy had on student learning. An ES of .40 has a high probability of supporting students in gaining one year's growth in one year's time.

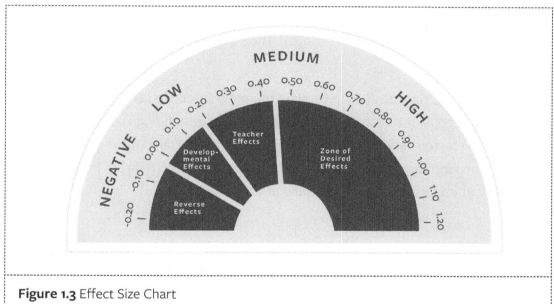

Figure 1.3 Effect Size Chart
Source: Adapted from Hattie, 2009.

Rigorous PBL centralizes key strategies from Hattie's original and subsequent studies of Visible Learning between 2009 and 2017. In particular, it highlights the following key factors that impact student learning:

❋ Clarity (ES .75)

❋ Feedback (ES .73)

✳ Assessment-Capable Learners (ES 1.44)

✳ Collective Teacher Efficacy (ES 1.23)

In 2021, the Visible Learning research was updated (and this update is ongoing) with additional studies and students. It confirmed the strength of these factors and illustrated the following updates:

✳ Clarity (ES .84)

✳ Feedback (ES .62)

✳ Assessment-Capable Learners (ES 1.33)

✳ Collective Teacher Efficacy (ES 1.36)

While the effect sizes have changed, the story of what makes a substantial impact remains the same.

Additionally, rigorous PBL leverages the most effective instructional strategies for surface, deep, and transfer levels of learning. Understanding these levels of complexity helps teachers and learners to parse out what they need most during different phases in the learning process. Table 1.1 illustrates strategies that are linked to a high probability of impact on student learning at each level.

Influence	Surface	Deep	Transfer
Outlining (ES .85)	X		
Similarities and differences across contexts (ES 1.32)			X
Seeking help from peers (ES .83)		X	
Classroom discussions (ES .82)		X	

Influence	Surface	Deep	Transfer
Mnemonics (ES .76)	X		
Seeing patterns in new situations (ES 1.14)			X
Strategies to integrate prior knowledge (e.g., KWL) (ES .93)	X		
Evaluation and reflection (ES .75)		X	
Solving problems in new situations (ES .80)			X

Table 1.1 Alignment of Strategies to Levels of Learning
ES = Effect Size
Source: Hattie & Donoghue, 2016.

Earlier, we mentioned the importance of impact; the aforementioned habits in Table 1.1 are derived from strategies that are likely to yield more than one year's growth in one year's time—when used at the right time. These strategies tend to have a higher impact at specific levels of learning. In other words, they are situational, requiring teachers to adapt their instruction to the level of complexity. We know, for example, that the utility of students making meaning through discussion when they have learned foundational principles is very different from asking students to debate a topic about which they still lack basic understanding. Likewise, using mnemonics to memorize key terms is an excellent way to learn surface knowledge. (How many of us remember Every Good Boy Does Fine, well into our adulthood?) Once deeper connections are made, mnemonics will do little to help students apply their learning. Rigor requires surface, deep, and transfer levels of learning; teaching in the rigorous PBL classroom requires habits of using the right strategy at the right time. The 15 habits outlined in this book are anchored to strategies that have a high probability of substantially increasing student learning.

The Impact of Rigorous PBL

Research released in 2021 confirmed that PBL can deliver on its promise (Saavedra et al., 2021; Krajcik et al., 2021; Duke et al., 2021; Deutscher et al., 2021). For instance, two large-scale randomized control studies, which encompassed more than 6,000 students in 124 diverse classrooms, found that rigorous project-based learning was an effective strategy for students. One of the studies, which took place in elementary schools, examined the impact of PBL in the science classroom (Krajcik 2021). The positive impact on student performance was evident for all student groups, including those at the lowest and highest reading levels. (See Figure 1.4.) Terada (2021) writes, "In a new study of 2,371 third-grade students, PBL raised average science test scores. Looking more closely, the data revealed that students at all reading levels outperformed their counterparts in traditional classrooms."

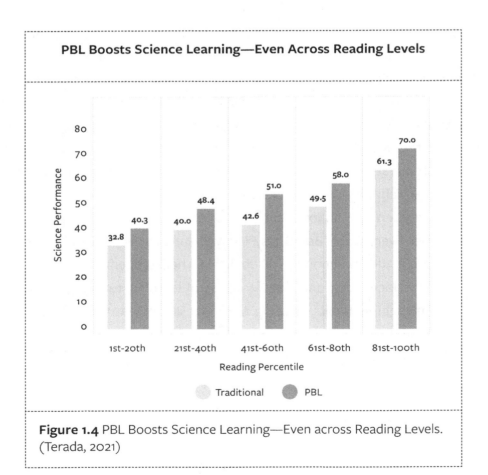

Figure 1.4 PBL Boosts Science Learning—Even across Reading Levels. (Terada, 2021)

It's important to note that more than 60% of the students involved in the elementary study qualified for free or reduced lunch and over half were students of color. This makes a compelling case for PBL in equity-minded schools.

The second study focused on high schoolers in Advanced Placement classes (Saavedra et al,. 2021). The results are impressive. (See Figure 1.5) Here is Terada (2021) again discussing the results of the Saaverdra et al. (2021) study:

Researchers found that nearly half of students in project-based classrooms passed their AP tests, outperforming students in traditional classrooms by 8 percentage points. Students from low-income households saw similar gains compared to their wealthier peers, making a strong case that well-structured PBL can be a more equitable approach than teacher-centered ones. Importantly, the improvements in teaching efficacy were both significant and durable: When teachers in the study taught the same curriculum for a second year, PBL students outperformed students in traditional classrooms by 10 percentage points.

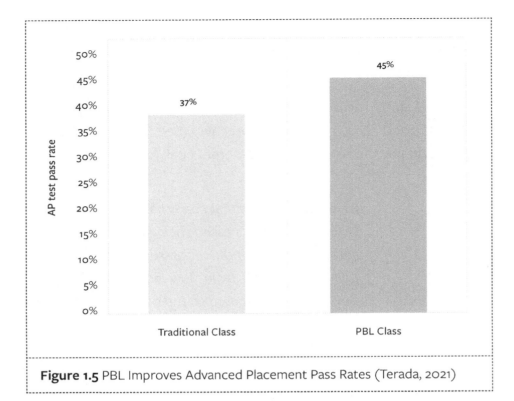

Figure 1.5 PBL Improves Advanced Placement Pass Rates (Terada, 2021)

These critical studies illustrate the point that when designed and implemented correctly, project-based learning can make a substantial impact on all students.

Other studies, including one in elementary school humanities classes, found that students in traditionally low-income, low-performing schools demonstrated five to six more months of growth in social studies and about two more months of growth in literacy achievement—specifically, informational reading—as compared to peers (Duke et al., 2021). Another study researched the efficacy of a sixth-grade project-based learning science course aligned to the Next Generation Science Standards (NGSS) and found students outperformed a comparison group by 11 percentage points on a science assessment developed as a measure of students' proficiencies with NGSS practices in the second year of implementation. Students also were found to transfer that success on state standardized tests in mathematics and English language arts. As a bonus, the study found student engagement improved.

Overall, recent research (Lucas Education Research, 2021) has illustrated that when PBL is designed and implemented in very specific, rigorous ways, academic growth is enhanced for all students. Our aim in this book is to put this research to work for you and your classroom in a low-plan, low-lift approach that has a high impact on all students. A summary of the impact shared in the Lucas Education Research (2021) brief is shown below.

Academic findings include:

✳ Adding rigorous PBL to Advanced Placement courses improved student achievement on AP exams.

✳ Elementary science students improved in science and areas of social and emotional learning with a project-based approach.

✳ Early elementary students using project-based learning made more progress in social studies and informational reading than peers in more traditional classrooms.

✳ Middle-school students outperformed their peers in science and other core subjects and improved in group work when using a project-based learning approach to science instruction. English language learners in the PBL classrooms also did better than a comparison group on a language proficiency test.

Equity-related findings include:

✳ High school students engaged in project-based learning in Advanced Placement US government and politics and environmental science courses outperformed students in traditional classrooms on AP exams. The effect was held for students from lower-income and higher-income households. Notably, a higher proportion of students in the study were from low-income households than is typical for AP test takers.

✳ Students participating in a PBL middle-school science program in high-poverty, diverse schools outperform peers receiving traditional science instruction on science, math, and English assessments. English learners in the PBL course outperformed peers on a language proficiency test.

✳ Third-grade students participating in a PBL science course did better on a science assessment than students in non-PBL classes. The assessment was aligned with Next Generation Science Standards and included items from state assessments. The positive impact of the PBL course on achievement held across racial, ethnic, and socioeconomic differences as well as reading ability levels.

✳ Second-grade students in low-income, low performing schools made five to six more months of learning gains in social studies with PBL instruction and two to three more months of gains in informational reading for the year as compared to peers.

Thinking Again with Rigorous PBL by Design

After five years of educators' testing Rigorous PBL by Design in classrooms and professional learning experiences around the world, many of the recommended strategies from *Rigorous PBL by Design* have deepened. At the same time, the authors have noticed inroads for nuance and a greater opportunity to leverage innovation. Shift happens when you focus on the action in the classroom! These changes are the result of research, practice, and the daily experiences of teachers, students, and leaders. While these changes are discussed throughout the book, a few have been highlighted below:

✳ Shifting from developing entry experiences that offer students one situation to creating entry experiences that often have multiple contexts

✳ Shifting from providing the learning intentions, success criteria, and driving questions to students to co-constructing each with students

※ Shifting from leveraging authentic audiences as the person or group that either "gives" the problem or "receives" the solution to embedding authentic audiences throughout the project as a value-added resource to learn new viewpoints within a context, develop a nuanced understanding of a subject area, and/or work through a problem

※ Shifting from keeping the problem and the problem conditions the same throughout the project to infusing greater authenticity into the PBL process by having students encounter changes in the project

※ Shifting from maintaining a general view of project-based learning to exploring its relationship to perspective taking and systems of power

※ Shifting from discussing rigorous PBL as it relates to the general population to including implications for exceptional learners

※ Shifting from building and implementing projects to investing in a set of habits that may be developed and implemented over time

In addition to these shifts, this text expands on teaching deep and transfer workshops, offering means for designing deep and transfer tasks, detailed strategies for giving and receiving feedback at deep and transfer levels, and approaches to assess student and teacher learning. This book will support teachers in engaging in that work by exploring how to design tasks, assessments, and daily lessons (termed *workshops* in the PBL classroom) at each level.

The intention is that a few years' time will necessitate a revised version of this book, laying out even more new learning, offering changes to previous thinking, and mitigating gaps that will assuredly be presented here. Dropping tools and picking up new ones can be hard, but if we focus on integrity of learning and not fidelity to a methodology, we should be able to handle such changes with a semblance of ease. Moreover, by questioning—and at times revising—our thinking, we will likely build better and more exciting pedagogical strategies within a contemporary framework.

Gearing Up for Rigorous Project Habits

This book follows a pattern frequently used in education. In this way, its sequence will seem familiar: plan the thing, do the thing, and then see what worked. But we urge readers to prioritize the doing of the thing, the action habits described in Chapters 3–6. This is, after all, where we succeed or fail, and try again, with students. Overall, this book explores 15 habits that will help teachers design, implement, and inspect. The following subsection provides an overview of the purpose, timing, and description of each set of habits.

RPBL Design

Planning ahead can help lay a path for building better habits. To prepare for implementation, a design template for problems and projects is provided. It is by no means the only template that can be used for this work; if there is a unit template that more closely fits the needs of the individual teacher or school, that format should take priority. The Rigorous PBL template is designed for a three-to-five-week unit of study (other templates may be found in the online Appendix).

Design Habits Rationale

Why? The design process ensures that a high level of clarity occurs for teachers and students throughout the project and that all levels of learning are addressed.

When? The design process occurs before a project begins. Projects are then adjusted throughout the project implementation process and at the conclusion of the project.

How? Teachers build a unit sequenced into four phases.

What? The design phase is based on four habits of design (see Table 1.2).

Rigorous PBL Teacher Design Habit	Success Criteria
Habit 1: **Make it clear** by creating student-friendly learning intentions and success criteria at surface, deep, and transfer levels of learning	Formulate learning intention(s) that are student friendly and written at the transfer level Design leveled success criteria at surface, deep, and transfer expectations
Habit 2: **See it (the learning) everywhere** by generating multiple contexts and one or more driving questions	Generate contexts across multiple fields, experiences, and student interests Develop one or more driving questions and align to surface and deep inquiry-based questions
Habit 3: **Plan for the right fit** by aligning tasks across surface, deep, and transfer expectations, and designing entry events, curveballs, and sequels for transfer	Align rigorous tasks with a variety of assessments across surface, deep, and transfer expectations Design transfer experiences, including entry events, curveballs, and sequels
Habit 4: **Lock it (the schedule) in** by setting tentative dates for workshops aligned to complexity levels	Determine the sequence for meeting transfer, deep, and surface outcomes Arrange and schedule workshops to meet surface, deep, and transfer outcomes on tentative dates Organize the design elements with a practical template

Table 1.2 RPBL Design Habits

RPBL Actions

The Rigorous PBL by Design methodology utilizes four main phases: project launch, surface-learning workshops, deep-learning workshops, and presentations and reflections (See Figure 1.6). Specific habits that teachers enact to successfully meet learning expectations are important in each phase. Each phase and habit is illuminated below.

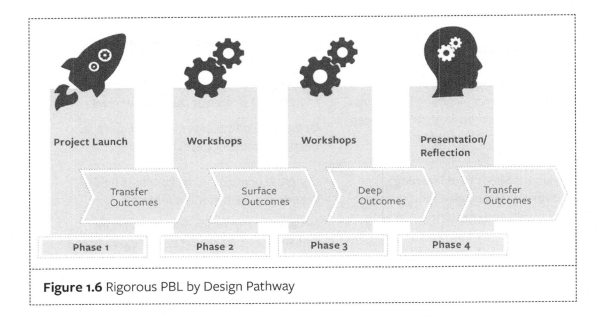

Figure 1.6 Rigorous PBL by Design Pathway

Phase 1 (Project Launch) Action Habits Rationale

Why? The project launch is built on the premise that students should encounter a set of real-world problems that ignites their engagement to solve challenging problems with others. This phase creates a rationale for learning new content and skills.

When? This phase is at the beginning of a rigorous PBL unit. It is an opportunity for students to explore a problem, generate questions, assess their current level of understanding, and devise a game plan for next steps.

How? Three high-impact strategies show up at the very beginning of the project and extend throughout: feedback, teacher clarity, and assessment capabilities. In addition, deep- and transfer-level strategies are embedded during this phase, including engaging in classroom discussions, seeking help from peers, seeing similarities and differences across contexts, and solving problems in unique contexts.

Students are introduced to problems or problem contexts and are assessed for their current knowledge and skills relative to the demands of the problem. Students then identify next steps through the next three phases of the project-based process.

Students also focus on the knowledge and skills they need to self-manage and engage in social contexts with others.

What? This phase is based on three key teacher habits. From the very beginning, the primary goal of these habits is to enable students to set a clear path for themselves and establish their purpose for learning (See Table 1.3).

Phase 1: Project Launch	
Rigorous PBL Teacher Habit	**Success Criteria**
Habit 5: **Start with a challenge** by setting your purpose with an entry event and getting students clear on what they're learning and what success looks like	~ Launch transfer-level expectations with a purposeful entry experience for all ~ Crystalize learning intentions, success criteria, and the driving question with students
Habit 6: **Name the gaps** by pre-assessing and discussing the results with students	~ Conduct a pre-assessment ~ Facilitate a discussion with students on their performance and next steps they can take via a protocol (ongoing criteria throughout the project)
Habit 7: **Look ahead** by creating next steps based on knows/need-to-knows and holding to learning agreements and protocols	~ Facilitate the Know/Need to Know list and create next steps ~ Hold to agreements and protocols that maximize the learning zone

Table 1.3 Project Launch Teacher Habits and Success Criteria during the Project Launch Phase

Phase 2 (Surface -Learning Workshops) Action Habits Rationale

Why? The building-knowledge phase is crucial, to ensure students build surface-level understanding of core content knowledge and skills to successfully meet underlying content standards and project demands.

When? This phase is typically the second phase of the four-part sequence. After the project launch, typically student need-to-knows are centered on questions related to surface-level expectations (e.g., defining, labeling, outlining, developing fluency).

How? Students participate in a series of lessons, often conducted through direct instruction. Students receive corrective feedback and complete daily tasks that require reading, writing, and talking. Teachers utilize strategies that include direct instruction along with high-impact learning strategies, including the use of mnemonics, outlining, and KWL charts (i.e., three-column tables that outline what a student knows [K], wants to know [W], and has learned [L]).

What? This phase is based on one key teacher habit related to surface-level learning. This habit is built on the premise that teachers and students have extensive experience in surface-level teaching and learning. This step is built on three success criteria (see Table 1.4).

Phase 2: Surface-Learning Workshops	
Rigorous PBL Teacher Habit	**Success Criteria**
Habit 8: **Build the foundation** by applying instructional and feedback strategies to support surface-level learning	~ Apply surface-level instruction to support student learning ~ Use appropriate feedback strategies to enhance student learning

Table 1.4 Teacher Habits and Success Criteria during the Surface-Learning Workshops Phase

Phase 3 (Deep-Learning Workshops) Action Habits Rationale

Why? Deep-learning workshops are part of making meaning. Students relate ideas and skills to form principles and enduring understanding of a discipline or set of disciplines.

When? This phase typically occurs after surface-level knowledge has been learned or while it's in the process of being learned.

How? Students are introduced to how concepts relate to one another through structured collaborative protocols and, in general, more open-ended tasks. Teachers take a more inquiry-based role using inquiry-based feedback, structured means for student communication, and tasks that require the convergence of ideas, such as concept maps and jigsaw.

What? The singular habit that composes Phase 3 is to question everything together. If ever a classroom were to sound noisy, this is the time. Student discourse thrives in this phase (see Table 1.5).

Phase 3: Deep-Learning Workshops	
Rigorous PBL Teacher Habit	**Success Criteria**
Habit 9: **Question everything together** through structured discussions, deep-level feedback strategies, and formative assessments	~ Use collaborative protocols to promote shared power and deep learning through engaging in classroom discussions that evaluate and reflect on knowledge and skills ~ Use deep-level feedback strategies to enhance student learning by reflecting on progress, determining next steps, and improving peer-to-peer feedback ~ Incorporate assessments (formative, two-thirds, and final) into the learning process to promote reflection

Table 1.5 Teacher Habits and Success Criteria during the Deep-Learning Workshops Phase

Phase 4 (Presentations and Reflections) Action Habits Rationale

Why? This phase is designed to ensure students apply their learning to real-world tasks, work with others, and can understand patterns across contexts. Its purpose is to ensure students are learning to transfer.

When? This phase is at the end of the process and in many ways mirrors the beginning of the unit. Both project launch (Phase 1) and presentations and reflections (Phase 4) are built for transfer learning.

How? Students are introduced to lessons that provide them with the knowledge and skills to transfer their learning, collaborate with others in structured teams, handle change and ambiguity, engage with authentic tasks and audiences to solve problems, and reflect on learning. Teachers utilize a blend of advocacy and inquiry to instruct and intervene with students in their learning.

What? This phase is based on three key teacher habits (see Table 1.6).

Phase 4: Presentations and Reflections	
Rigorous PBL Teacher Habit	**Success Criteria**
Habit 10: **Return to transfer** by implementing transfer-level workshops to apply learning in real-world contexts and address curveballs	~ Revisit the entry experience, driving questions, learning intentions, and success criteria to determine key knows/need-to-knows ~ Engage individually or in small teams to address the driving question ~ Implement transfer-level workshops to support student learning in how to apply their learning in real-world contexts, problems, and products ~ Engage students in curveballs (perspective, situation, content)
Habit 11: **Deliver on the challenge** by structuring means for showcasing work and giving/receiving feedback and engaging students in project sequels	~ Structure means for showcasing work and giving/receiving feedback to/from others ~ Engage students in project sequels

Phase 4: Presentations and Reflections	
Rigorous PBL Teacher Habit	**Success Criteria**
Habit 12: **Look in the mirror** by conducting reflective protocols on academic growth, meeting cultural expectations, and addressing the driving question	~ Conduct reflective protocols on academic growth, meet cultural expectations, and address the driving questions

Table 1.6 Teacher Habits and Success Criteria during the Presentations and Reflections Phase

RPBL Inspection

Action, without reflection, is short lived. The inspection habits recommended in this book are meant to make inspecting our impact habitual. The final three motion habits make using evidence central to informing the impact of our habits and the efficacy of implementation. Moreover, they are doable problem-solving strategies to inspect and move back to action in a short time.

Inspection Habits Rationale

Why? To sustain the pursuit of improving our impact, our habit development and refinement, and our innovation in contemporary methodologies.

When? While inspecting our impact occurs throughout a unit of study, this phase resides at the conclusion of our work.

How? Teachers use a rapid inquiry-based process and engage with colleagues to determine impact, discover refinement or opportunities for change, and design next steps.

What? This phase is based on three key habits. They require safe and supportive relationships with colleagues and a willingness to continually refine our practices. (See Table 1.7)

Rigorous PBL Teacher Design Habit	Success Criteria
Habit 13: **Make discourse deliberate** by agreeing to shared values and behaviors for shared work and following through on them	~ Agree to shared values and assumptions and behaviors for shared work ~ Follow through on shared values, assumptions, and behaviors
Habit 14: **Sprint** by adhering to a rapid improvement process	~ Adhere to a rapid improvement process
Habit 15: **Choose action** by implementing a personalized plan for improving habits	~ Implement a personalized plan for improving habits ~ Incorporate deliberate deviations in practice

Table 1.7 Inspection Teacher Habits and Success Criteria during Implementation

Conclusion

The aforementioned habits are critical for teachers and students to implement in the classroom. The following chapters walk through each phase and offer concrete examples, tools, and strategies to support practitioners in building habits. Prior to exploring those in-class action habits, the next chapter will present a means for designing rigorous PBL through simple templates that can be modified based on teacher needs.

Review Questions

※ Review the key lessons or takeaways in the Introduction and Chapter 1. What lesson stands out for you? Why?

﹡ Review the project habits in the Introduction and Chapter 1. What habits surprised you? What habits are you familiar with? How will you go after the surprising habits? How will you find nuance in habits that are already familiar?

﹡ Which habits in Figure 0.2 stand out as the most challenging to implement in your classroom? How will you begin to bring those habits into your classroom?

﹡ To what extent are you already engaging in the phases, steps, and habits outlined in this chapter?

﹡ If you were to focus on a few action habits for the next few months, what would you focus on? How would you stick to those action habits?

﹡ What are your key questions to begin the work of bringing *The Project Habit* to life in your classroom?

﹡ Why have these action habits been nonexistent in your classroom? What might be your next steps? Which phase seems the most challenging to implement? What will you do to lower the challenge threshold to implement the aforementioned habits?

﹡ With the exception of Phase 2, what phase will you focus your time, energy, and effort on? What excites you about the phase you have selected?

Next Steps

﹡ Review the Introduction and Chapter 1 along with the reflective questions with colleagues. Use a structured protocol (e.g., Final Word and Four A's; both protocols can be found in the online Appendix) to discuss these chapters.

﹡ Review your key questions along with the habits you are looking to develop. Create a set of next steps you will take to learn about and implement the habits. To assist here, please review Chapter 7 (Tables 7.6 and 7.7) for ways to make each of the habits doable in your class. As you review the chapters, select a habit you will implement and sustain over time.

Chapter 2

RIGOROUS PBL: PLANNING

" Let's focus on the action rather than the intention. The power of formative lies in the moment.

—Dylan Wiliam

It's no secret that for rigorous learning to come alive in our classrooms, we need a plan. Like scheduling a time in the day to exercise, those moments when we will leverage high-impact strategies need a distinct place in our lessons and unit plans. Taking time in advance to design opportunities to strengthen clarity, feedback, and assessment-capable learning will make it more likely that we act on those opportunities when we're in the classroom. Planning is an investment in action.

But what happens when our best-laid plans meet actual students? For the students in the classroom featured in Figure 2.1, the teacher has planned well and focused on ensuring everyone is clear on learning expectations. Despite those plans, student 1 is focused on the context of the unit (slime) and student 2 is focused on the learning outcomes (the transitions among solids, liquids, and gasses). Research would tell us that student 2 will likely have a better chance of tracking his own learning, giving and receiving accurate feedback, and transferring what he learns across contexts. For example, when he encounters the way water transitions between physical states, he will be able to relate that to what he learned during the slime activity. Both students heard the same instruction from their teacher, but one still remains fixated on the activity rather than the learning.

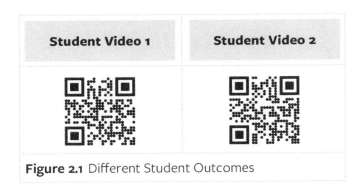

Figure 2.1 Different Student Outcomes

The key to ensuring all students learn is how the teacher responds to students in the class. Regardless of our best-laid plans, it is our habits in the moment with students that matter most. That said, we do need to plan—and this chapter highlights how to plan for surface, deep, and transfer learning and sequence those levels of complexity into a project. Here we propose guidelines for building the right habits for planning a Rigorous PBL by Design unit, knowing that, above all, our charge is to be responsive to the reality of learners.

We urge the reader to plan quickly, seek feedback, begin implementation, and then make adjustments to the plan on the go. One key lesson the authors have learned is that any unit of study designed in isolation becomes brittle when introduced to students. Units may be designed with a context that we're certain students will love, only to fall flat or to be too far over their heads upon project launch. Sometimes, even after a project is in full swing, questions need to be redrafted. Student prior knowledge may require more or fewer scaffolds than originally planned for. Adjustments are always required, and they are a sign that the teacher is being responsive to the learners in the room. Moreover, the best units are those that have the flexibility to incorporate student input throughout. Design with intent; implement with freedom.

During Rigorous PBL by Design workshops, we call the unit design process the "etching in sand" because we are simply drafting a unit that will change and shift over time. We focus on designing for clarity, challenge, and the cultural components that are necessary and then ensure there is enough flexibility to make adjustments throughout the unit.

This chapter walks through the steps necessary to create a unit of study. Templates are provided as a way to structure the design process and fully engage in the four habits shown in Table 2.1.

Rigorous PBL Teacher Design Habit	Success Criteria
Habit 1: **Make it clear** by creating student-friendly learning intentions and success criteria at surface, deep, and transfer levels of learning	~ Formulate learning intention(s) that are student friendly and written at the transfer level ~ Design leveled success criteria at surface, deep, and transfer expectations
Habit 2: **See it (the learning) everywhere** by generating multiple contexts and one or more driving questions	~ Generate contexts across multiple fields, experiences, and student interests ~ Develop one or more driving questions and align to surface and deep inquiry-based questions
Habit 3: **Plan for the right fit** by aligning tasks across surface, deep, and transfer expectations, and designing entry events, curveballs, and sequels for transfer	~ Align rigorous tasks with a variety of assessments across surface, deep, and transfer expectations ~ Design transfer experiences, including entry events, curveballs, and sequels for students to encounter at the transfer level of learning

Rigorous PBL Teacher Design Habit	Success Criteria
Habit 4: **Lock it (the schedule) in** by setting tentative dates for workshops aligned to complexity levels	~ Determine the sequence for meeting transfer, deep, and surface outcomes ~ Arrange and schedule workshops to meet surface, deep, and transfer outcomes on tentative dates ~ Use an easy-to-use template for organizing the design elements

Table 2.1 Key Steps for Building Rigorous PBL by Design Units

 *Habit 1:* **Make it clear** *by creating student-friendly learning intentions and success criteria at surface, deep, and transfer levels of learning*

We know that teachers are doing great things in the classroom. Teachers are usually pretty clear on what they expect from their students. The key is to ensure that students are with us when we are doing what we're doing. In other words, we need to make sure that our clarity is translating to students. The following habit incorporates two key success criteria to support teachers in designing for student clarity. Beyond these criteria, a practitioner's note has been added to provide additional texture to designing for clarity.

Success Criteria: *Formulate learning intention(s) that are student friendly and written at the transfer level*

The first step in the design process is to identify the learning intentions (i.e., state or national standard) that students are expected to learn in the next several weeks. If a teacher has multiple outcomes, then they need to simply repeat the following process for each outcome.

We are working to refine the learning intentions to a digestible sentence that makes sense to students in the classroom. To do this, we need to reorient them into student-friendly language. The following scaffold is helpful in reorienting the standard to a student perspective (see Table 2.2).

Start with including a verb that orients students to a future goal they will be aiming to achieve. Stems such as "I will," "I can," "I should," and "to what extent" are examples of ways to begin the transformation of a standard to a learning goal.

Next, include a transfer verb to set expectations for students to reach transfer-level expectations. Transfer verbs include *apply, present, generalize,* and *hypothesize.*

Finally, include the learning outcome of the standard. This may include writing persuasively, solving multistep equations, or discerning the strengths and weaknesses of democracy.

Learning Intention Components	Elementary Example	Secondary Example
Stem	I will . . .	I should . . .
Transfer verb	Predict	Present
Learning outcome	CCSS.MATH. CONTENT.3.N.F.A.3. Explain equivalence of fractions in special cases, and compare fractions by reasoning about their size	HS-LS1-5 From molecules to organisms: Structures and Processes Use a model to illustrate how photosynthesis transforms light energy into stored chemical energy
Putting it all together	I will predict solutions to real problems that require me to compare different types of fractions	I will apply my understanding of photosynthesis to an existing or future problem

Table 2.2 Learning Intentions Examples

Notice that there is no mention of a task/activity or a context. This is a critical part of this habit and is essential for keeping students focused on the learning and ensuring potential transfer.

Success Criteria: *Design leveled success criteria at surface, deep, and transfer expectations*

People like knowing what's expected of them. "How will I know if I'm doing it right?" is a natural question we ask ourselves in schools, boardrooms, and Zoom meetings. In fact, clear goals are frequently lauded as a vital component of job satisfaction. To ensure that success is not a mystery for learners in the classroom, it helps to sketch out success criteria in advance. Simply write out what success looks like at surface, deep, and transfer levels. Specifying the complexity levels of success criteria helps to do two things. First, it ensures that as teachers, we are headed in the direction of rigor, which incorporates all three levels. Second, these can become a valuable touch-point for students who are prone to lump all learning together and determine that they've either got it or they don't—rather than seeing a pathway for next steps. The most efficient way to do this is to use the SOLO taxonomy verbs in Table 2.3. The RPBL template contains a success criteria table in which these can be neatly mapped out.

Rubric Complexity		
Surface	Deep	Transfer
~ Name ~ Tell ~ Rename ~ Define ~ Describe who, what, where, when, or how ~ Identify ~ Recall ~ Recite ~ Reorganize ~ Label ~ Locate ~ Match ~ Measure ~ Solve one misstep ~ Use rules ~ List several examples ~ Describe and explain using context ~ Give examples and non-examples ~ Perform a procedure	~ Cite supporting evidence ~ Organize ~ Outline ~ Interpret ~ Revise for meaning ~ Explain connections ~ Compare ~ Contrast ~ Synthesize ~ Verify ~ Show cause and effect ~ Analyze ~ Argue ~ Assess ~ Deconstruct ~ Draw conclusions ~ Extend patterns ~ Infer ~ Predict ~ Solve nonroutine problems	~ Reorganize into new structure ~ Formulate ~ Generalize ~ Produce and present ~ Design and conduct ~ Collaborate ~ Evaluate across contexts ~ Critique ~ Hypothesize ~ Initiate ~ Reflect ~ Research ~ Compare and contrast across contexts

Table 2.3 Levels of Learning Based on the SOLO Taxonomy
Source: Biggs & Collins, 1982.

Two examples of success criteria are provided below (see Table 2.4). Notice that there is no mention of a task/activity, nor is there a context in the success criteria. This is a critical part of this habit and is essential for keeping students focused on the learning and ensuring potential transfer.

Learning Goal Components	Surface	Deep	Transfer
Example 1 CCSS.MATH. CONTENT.3.N.F.A.3. Explain equivalence of fractions in special cases, and compare fractions by reasoning about their size	~ Describe how two fractions are equivalent based on size and/or number line ~ Recognize equivalent fractions ~ Explain why fractions are equivalent ~ List examples of equivalent fractions	~ Compare two fractions with the same numerator or denominator ~ Analyze fractions using a visual fraction model	~ Critique solutions to real-world problems and solutions ~ Design and conduct an experiment using equivalence of fractions across different contexts
Example 2 HS-LS1-5 From molecules to organisms: Structures and Processes Use a model to illustrate how photosynthesis transforms light energy into stored chemical energy	~ Define photosynthesis ~ List various organisms that photosynthesize (outside of plants) ~ Describe inputs and outputs of matter and transfer	~ Compare and contrast models of photosynthesis including diagrams, chemical equations, and conceptual models	~ Create a metaphor that applies the concept and process of photosynthesis ~ Hypothesize a real-world problem that involves the concept and process of photosynthesis

Table 2.4 Leveled Success Criteria

Connection to exceptional learners: Clear success criteria benefit all learners, including those who are multilingual or neurodivergent. At school, emerging English learners are bombarded by a language in which they are not yet fluent; it can quickly lead to cognitive overload. When there are so many new words and syntax patterns to process, being clear about where to focus can prevent overwhelm. Additionally, when the time is taken to name success criteria at all levels (not just the end product or transfer), students who need support see that even surface-level success criteria are a valid first step on the path to deeper learning. Leveled success criteria take the mystery out of what's most important to focus on and help to make the overall learning intention more approachable for all learners.

When planning for a project that will extend over multiple weeks, sometimes it makes sense to work with more than one learning intention. For example, will students be learning how to predict velocity and also how to write a lab report? Or will students be learning standards that are specific literature and informational texts simultaneously? In these cases, learning intentions are more likely to be clear if they are separate. Based on the work in *Teaching for Transfer* (McDowell, 2020), the recommendation in this situation is to integrate transfer-level outcomes across intentions. In this way, the success criteria look like those in Table 2.5.

Learning Intention: I will analyze how plot, setting, and characters affect the theme	Learning Intention: I will research an issue by closely reading multiple texts
Surface ~ Name the major characters ~ Describe the setting ~ Explain the plot	Surface ~ Identify the main idea of what I read ~ Tell someone about the most interesting part of the text ~ Define new words in what I read
Deep ~ Cite textual evidence to support analysis of characters and setting ~ Relate plot, characters, and setting to the overall theme	Deep ~ Cite evidence that supports the main idea and details ~ Explain connections between this text and current events
Transfer Compare and contrast the themes in a fictional text with current, real-world events	
Table 2.5 Learning Intentions and Leveled Success Criteria	

Practitioner's Note: *Scrub away all tasks, activities, and contexts from learning outcomes and success criteria.*

Review the learning outcomes and success criteria as they are written and make sure that task/activities and contexts are absent. Having a colleague review your work is helpful here.

Students need to understand what success looks like to meet the goal. As such, we need to draft the specific learning outcomes and success criteria for what intentions students need to achieve and how they reach the goal. It is critical in the design process that students are shown only what they need to know or do in order to meet the goal. As such, activities/tasks and contexts should not appear in the outcomes and success criteria. The examples and nonexamples below may support you and your team in ensuring you don't drift into context-rich learning intentions (see additional examples of learning intentions and success criteria in the online Appendix). This approach supports students in tracking their progress, giving and receiving feedback, and transferring their learning across contexts (see Table 2.6).

Example	Nonexample
I will present a new narrative in which the minority perspective becomes the dominant perspective.	I will read Chapter 7 of our history textbook, complete the graphic organizer, and rewrite it from the Navajo point of view.
I will apply the formula for volume to predict how many units will fill a given space.	I will watch the video with my class and predict how many bottles of soda it will take to fill the swimming pool.

Table 2.6 Examples and Nonexamples of Learning Intentions with and without Contexts

Note for exceptional learners: Maintaining high expectations while assessing fairly in the mainstream classroom can present challenges to teachers who teach exceptional learners. Students who require special education services or language support may achieve the same success criteria as their peers, but they need to show it in a different way. Getting to success criteria that is squeaky clean can help separate an accessible goal from an inaccessible task. For example, a student can show that they're able to define key terms by using nonlinguistic representation instead of completing definitions on a quiz. A student who struggles to write may be able to describe main ideas and details with a verbal summary, rather than a written one.

Sample leveled success criteria may be found in the online Appendix. You may also want to review Table 2.2 and the sample projects in the online Appendix.

Practitioner's Note: *Facts aren't the only thing. But they're an important thing. In our impetus to drive students toward transfer, it is tempting to focus on skill alone as we develop success criteria. While the connection between skills and transfer is thought to be straightforward, the reality is that basic knowledge is vital for transfer to occur. You simply can't think critically about a subject or topic you don't know anything about. For instance, asking students to conduct an analysis on historical documents is going to require students to understand the history knowledge in* *those documents, or they will be unable to effectively analyze. As such, the link between what students can do (procedural skills) and what they know (declarative knowledge) is important to consider.*

We have to move beyond tasking students with developing the skill of writing a five-sentence paragraph in the hope they can apply it to solve a local problem. Yes, they likely will be able to transfer that skill, but to what level of success? We encourage teachers to develop students' developing declarative knowledge alongside procedural skills.

The value of declarative knowledge, or facts, is perhaps best documented in studies about reading comprehension. Wexler (2019) argues that by overfocusing on reading skills, rather than knowledge, we exacerbate the already significant gap between students who come from low-income homes and those with more resources. Similarly, Daniel Willingham (2021) has written extensively about the abundance of evidence that facts precede skill, especially when it comes to reading. Put simply, when we read about something we are familiar with, we are more likely to remember and apply it. The implication from both authors is that including basic facts in our criteria for success is essential to support students in making connections and, ultimately, transferring their knowledge and skills to a new situation.

 *Habit 2:* **See it (the learning)** *everywhere by generating multiple contexts and one or more driving questions*

Success Criteria: *Generate contexts across multiple fields, experiences, and student interests*

One of the distinct differences between general PBL and rigorous PBL is the generation and use of multiple contexts. This approach aims to get students into the habit of applying what they learn to more than one situation. Routinely posing questions such as "How does what I know apply here? What makes one complex situation slightly different from another, and how are they the same?" gets students and teachers into the habit of seeing their learning everywhere.

To start, brainstorm a number of situations/contexts that relate to your learning outcome. A simple way to do this is to create a list in your notebook, or work with colleagues to build a list using sticky notes. Teachers also may want to survey students for what they already know about the outcome and how they see it applies in their lives. This technique is particularly useful for teachers striving to build culturally relevant contexts—students can help the teacher think outside the box of her own cultural roots. Examples of multiple contexts are given in Table 2.7.

Example Learning Intentions and Grade-Level Spans	Context Ideas
I will predict solutions to authentic problems by comparing different types of fractions.	~ Following a recipe ~ Medical prescriptions ~ Fitness (e.g., body mass index) ~ Image ratios
I will analyze how plot, setting, and characters affect the theme.	~ Multiple genres ~ Multiple settings (e.g., *Farewell to Manzanar* and *They Called Us Enemy*) ~ Grimms vs. contemporary tales ~ Different perspectives (e.g., Grendel, *A Tale of Two Beasts*)
I will research an issue by closely reading multiple texts.	~ Genetic modification ~ Religious freedom ~ Selective admissions ~ Critical race theory
I will apply my understanding of photosynthesis to an existing or future problem.	~ Carbon sequestration ~ Agricultural development ~ Photochemical switches and electronics ~ Medicine (e.g., light-induced tissue damage)

Table 2.7 RPBL Context Examples

Practitioner's Note: *Make sure contexts are accessible for all students.*

Culturally relevant pedagogy is a framework for ensuring educators uphold students' cultural identities while at the same time challenging societal inequalities. TThis is accomplished when students are supported in developing positive ethnic and social identities regarding their own culture and that of others. Students' critical consciousness- their ability to recognize, critique, and take action to address social inequities- can be coupled with with the Rigorous PBL by Design shifts, which include clarity, challenge, and a learning-centered culture. While other design elements in rigorous PBL focus on developing academic capacity, building a learning-centered culture, and problem-solving, this part of the design process focuses on creating space for students' identities within the classroom. We urge readers to consider Zaretta Hammond's argument that culture is the way every brain makes sense of the world. There may be many languages, styles of dress, and ethnic backgrounds represented in a classroom—a reflection of "surface culture" (Hammond, 2015) that may offer a jumping-off point for relevant contexts. But it is also valuable to connect across points of "deep culture," such as notions of fairness and definitions of kinship, that unite—rather than distinguish—different students in a classroom. It is critical for teachers to evaluate the following questions:

❋ To what extent am I including contexts that will affirm the cultural values of my students and those of others?

❋ To what extent will the contexts I'm exploring provide students with the ability to approach real-world problems that also help us improve human dignity and equality?

When brainstorming contexts, consider the following:

❋ What cultural values and identities are present in my classroom?

❋ How can we solve real-world problems in ways that honor our collective need for belonging and dignity?

❋ What are key questions that students are *presently* interested in?

Success Criteria: *Develop one or more driving questions and align to surface and deep inquiry-based questions*

A driving question is a transfer-level question that students are attempting to answer through the project. This question requires surface and deep knowledge and may cross multiple contexts. Sample driving questions include:

* ❋ To what extent should children suffer to protect unvaccinated adults?

* ❋ When should individualist cultures borrow from the norms of collectivist cultures?

* ❋ Where can teenagers most effectively enhance the social and emotional well-being of young children?

* ❋ To what extent is there space to find common ground on issues of equity, diversity, and inclusion via social media platforms?

Two approaches to creating driving questions are presented below (see examples in Table 2.8):

Approach 1: Transform the learning outcome into a question

Approach 2: Facilitate student-generated driving questions

1. **Single context:** Give students one situation. Ask them to generate their own driving question using a protocol that elicits multiple perspectives from peers, such as Four A's, Final Word, or interviews (see the online Appendix).

2. **Multiple contexts:** Use matrices of multiple contexts for students to generate a question. One particularly powerful strategy to support this level of learning is the jigsaw (see a detailed description of the protocol in the online Appendix).

	Approach 1	Approach 2 (Single Context)	Approach 2 (Multiple Contexts)
Step 1	State the learning intention.	Provide students with an article on the efficiencies and inefficiencies of agricultural development.	Provide students with multiple contexts: ~ Genetic modification ~ Religious freedom ~ Selective admissions ~ Critical race theory
Step 2	Use one of the following stems: To what extent . . . Should . . . When . . . Where . . .	Students use a protocol to discuss the article and identify what they may be learning.	Ask students to work in groups to find the theme or connection between the various contexts. In addition, ask students to identify the potential goal and success criteria.
Step 3	Convert to a question: To what extent can I predict solutions to authentic problems by comparing different types of fractions?	Show students the actual learning intention and success criteria.	Show students the actual learning intention and success criteria.
Step 4	Add context: To what extent can I predict solutions that will help children to manage their weight and prevent obesity?	Ask students to compare and contrast their generated learning intentions and success criteria to the teacher-created criteria.	Ask students to compare and contrast their generated learning intentions and success criteria to the teacher-created criteria.

Table 2.8 Two Approaches to Create the Driving Question

Note: Our second approach, in which students co-construct the driving question, is discussed at length in Chapter 3 via Habit 5.

Habit 3: **Plan for the right fit** *by aligning tasks across surface, deep, and transfer expectations; and designing entry events, curveballs, and sequels for transfer*

When designing activities and assessments for students to meet surface, deep, and transfer expectations, the following considerations should be made:

✳ Assessments may be conducted using an unobtrusive, obtrusive, or student-generated approach.

✳ Tasks should involve reading, writing, and/or talking.

✳ Assessments and tasks should be aligned to surface, deep, and transfer levels.

Success Criteria: *Align rigorous tasks with a variety of assessments across surface, deep, and transfer expectations*

It's common to hear the word *assessment* and expect to turn to the end of a chapter for the quiz or midterm exam. In reality, formative assessments are far more valuable to change the course of learning than the more traditional summatives we utilize at the end of a unit. One popular analogy is "Summative assessments happen when the chef serves the soup. Formative assessments are every time the chef tastes the soup to see what she needs to add." Assessment should happen not only at the end of a project but throughout.

A variety of assessment types exist; some of them, like unobtrusive assessments, may never appear in a gradebook. But if they are gauging where students are in their learning and helping the learners and teacher plan their next step, they are as valuable as any paper-and-pencil quiz.

Once the design habit of designing success criteria across surface, deep, and transfer levels has been actualized, aligning corresponding assessments is a logical next step. A variety of assessment types can demonstrate students' progress at surface, deep, and transfer. Obtrusive, unobtrusive, and student-generated assessments can all be valuable methods for helping students—and teachers—measure progress. Each is defined below:

※ **Obtrusive assessments** are assessments in which instruction and learning are interrupted to demonstrate knowledge. Obtrusive assessments include paper-and-pencil tests, demonstrations, and performances.

※ **Unobtrusive assessments** are assessments in which instruction and learning are not interrupted while performing an assessment.

※ **Student-generated assessments** are learning tasks in which students present what they are learning to others.

	Obtrusive	Unobtrusive	Student Generated
Language arts	The teacher assigns a persuasive essay in which students make a claim about a topic of their choice and support it with appropriate facts and qualifiers. Students begin the task in class and turn the assignment in the next day.	A teacher observes a student writing a haiku poem of his or her own design. The teacher considers this an unobtrusive assessment of the student's ability to write this type of poem.	To demonstrate her understanding of a book read in class, a fifth-grade student proposes that she write a paper describing the events of the story and how one caused another, leading to the story's ultimate resolution.

	Obtrusive	Unobtrusive	Student Generated
Mathematics	The teacher gives students four objects each. They must consider the weight of each object and write down estimations they consider to be reasonable, using the units of measure studied in class. They must also write brief justifications for their answers. At the end of class, the students turn in their assessments.	A teacher observes a student working a division problem from a homework assignment on the board. The student works through the problem correctly, and the teacher considers this an unobtrusive assessment of the student's ability to perform the process of division.	To demonstrate his understanding of geometric angles, a fourth grader proposes that he measure and draw accurate obtuse and right angles as well as complementary and supplementary angles in the presence of the teacher.

Table 2.9 Assessment Examples
Source: Marzano, 2009.

Each type of assessment is beneficial for determining student performance and then identifying what to do with that data. The data could be used as feedback for the teacher, for the student, or to report student performance as a means of summative assessment. Table 2.10 provides assessment examples of each type of assessment at surface, deep, and transfer. See the online Appendix for additional examples of assessments for deep and transfer learning.

	Obtrusive	Unobtrusive	Student Generated
Surface	Students define key vocabulary terms in an online quiz.	Student responses to class-wide discussion are noted by the teacher.	Students generate a study guide with the key questions they believe are critical for developing surface knowledge.
Deep	Students are stopped in the middle of a protocol to address specific questions. The responses may come from written responses, oral presentations, or discussion prompts on Google Classroom or Canvas.	Students are observed engaging in group discussions, or writing, to tackle deep level tasks.	Students generate a probing question and choose a discussion protocol. They use priming questions to answer key need-to-knows that were generated by students and aligned to the success criteria.
Transfer	Students are assessed through their performance on a transfer task. Assessments include performance tasks, GRASPS problems, Four Act Tasks, and matrix problems.	The teacher catches students' interactions with group members, authentic audiences, and individual actions during performance.	Students use the GRASPS framework and create a new problem within a different context that aligns with the success criteria.

Table 2.10 Assessment Examples of Surface, Deep, and Transfer Levels

In Rigorous PBL by Design (McDowell, 2017), it was argued that project design must incorporate reading, writing, and talking. Moreover, we argue that practitioners should take deliberate steps to ensure that the reading, writing, and talking are happening across surface, deep, and transfer levels. Table 2.11 showcases examples at each level of learning. As you consider the types of assessments appropriate at each stage of learning, keep in mind that the way students process and demonstrate learning extends beyond obtrusive assessments.

	Surface	Deep	Transfer
Reading	Preview a passage and highlight key ideas	Place annotations when key inferences about relationships and principles become apparent	Find other texts that draw on similar inferences and principles from a different context
Writing	List and describe key ideas	Construct a thesis statement that depicts the relationship between key ideas	Write an opinion piece
Talking	Recite key ideas	Argue the key principles and inferences from a passage	Argue how the key principles and inferences from the class-based passage relate to a new context in front of a panel

Table 2.11 Rigorous PBL by Design
Source: McDowell, 2017, p. 62.

> **Connection to multilingual learners:** Students who are learning academic English and speak a different language (or languages) at home build English proficiency by practicing across the four language domains: reading, writing, listening, and speaking. Each is foundational to building fluency in receptive and productive language in an academic setting. When we are deliberate about building in time to read, write, and speak across complexity levels, we can curb the tendency to water down instruction into a cycle of passive listening and short, one-word discourse. We want to give students just as much opportunity to produce language about their learning as they have to receive and understand information.

Deep-Learning Tasks and Assessments

Priming, Protocols, and Probing

If we know that the vast majority of classroom discourse remains at the surface level, then we also know that planning in advance for deep learning is a habit worth cultivating. Deep learning is largely driven by peer-to-peer feedback, classroom discussions, and evaluation and reflection. This interactive work could be around ideas, tasks, or problems. For example, students may evaluate why vaccine mandates are contentious to Americans, or why certain forms of writing inspire while others are rather dull. They may discuss why the solution to a math problem is correct, or why the performance on one task warrants a B+ whereas another work sample warrants a B-. The following three deep-learning approaches are ways to engage in this work:

❋ **Priming:** Ask questions that center students on the core principles or practices of a discipline or disciplines.

❋ **Protocols:** Structure a conversation in a way for students to engage in effective discussions that may relate to evaluating ideas, tasks, or problems, reflecting on the work of others or their own work and giving and receiving feedback.

❋ **Probing:** Use stimulating questions to deepen—and at times to sustain—peer-to-peer feedback, classroom discussions, and evaluations and reflections.

Examples of each are provided in Table 2.12.

Priming	Protocols	Probing
~ Why do they hate us? ~ Do we all "have a code" that we live by? What makes up that code? ~ Why did Picasso paint *Guernica*, and what does it tell us about today? ~ What makes a good artist? ~ What might prevent another 9/11? ~ What makes a great speaker great? ~ Can you predict the future?	~ Final Word ~ In2Out ~ Harkness protocol ~ Socratic seminar ~ Discussion mapping ~ Four A's	~ What do you mean by ____? ~ Why? ~ Can you elaborate? Tell me more. ~ Could you rephrase that? I don't understand your point. ~ Could you give me an example or an analogy to explain that? ~ How does this relate to ____? ~ What other perspectives emerge for you? ~ Do I understand you to be saying ____? ~ Why do you think that? ~ What's your evidence? What's your reasoning? ~ But earlier, didn't we say that ____, which seems to be at odds with what you're saying now? Can you clarify? ~ I disagree. Convince me. ~ How would you respond to those who say ____? ~ Who has a completely different idea or reason? ~ Is it really either-or? Might there be different "right" answers or ways of thinking about this?

Table 2.12 Priming, Protocols, and Probing Examples
Source: Adapted from McTighe & Wiggins, 2013.

Each of these deep-learning situations utilizes dialogue to make meaning of information. Reading and writing go hand in hand to complement these strategies. Reading beforehand will prepare students for the discussion; reading afterward may be necessary to seek further answers or information. Writing also serves to bolster deep-learning protocols before or after. Examples of writing may include completing reflective journals, writing an essay, and annotating a text.

Connection to multilingual learners: Quality interactions are essential to support deep conceptual and language learning (Billings & Mueller, n.d.). All students—and multilingual learners in particular—benefit from the sustained dialogue that is characteristic of quality interactions. Sustained dialogue is open ended and solicits more than just a one-sentence answer. When teachers use priming, protocols, and probing techniques, multilingual learners stand to develop their language skills in the context of deep discourse about concepts. Table tents and reference sheets with sentence stems that help students contribute to, and build on, the discussion are helpful scaffolds for any of the protocols listed above.

Transfer-Learning Tasks

In the same way that planning for deep learning should become habitual for teachers, planning for transfer is just as necessary. Transfer learning is best accomplished through open-ended performance tasks. A performance task is any learning activity or assessment that requires students to perform by demonstrating their knowledge, understanding, and proficiency. Performance tasks are not all inherently transferred. At a surface level, for example, students could apply specific knowledge, like how to kick a ball. Yet for transfer learning, students need to apply their understanding within or across different contexts (e.g., playing soccer—demonstrating kicking skills alongside other skills of the game, or combining kicking and other offensive and defensive strategies in kickball or football).

To qualify as a high-quality performance task, Jay McTighe and Chris Gareis (2021) state that performance tasks call for students to (1) apply their learning in some context, and (2) explain what they have done. Whether a task calls for a written response (e.g., an academic essay or blog post), a spoken response (e.g., an audio recording or a live debate), or a visual or physical communication (e.g., an infographic or an interpretive dance), students need to convey their reasoning, justify their decisions, and support their interpretations.

As such, transfer-level performance tasks

- ✳ call for the application of knowledge and skills, not just recall or recognition;

- ✳ are open ended and typically do not yield a single, correct answer;

- ✳ establish authentic contexts for performance;

- ✳ provide evidence of understanding via transfer;

- ✳ are multifaceted;

- ✳ integrate two or more subjects or 21st century skills; and

- ✳ utilize established criteria and rubrics.

Moreover, McTighe and Gareis (2021) argue that for such performance tasks to be deemed transferable, they must place students in situations that are

new to the student or situations containing new elements as compared to the situation in which the abstraction was learned. . . . Ideally, we are seeking a problem which will test the extent to which an individual has learned to apply the abstraction in a practical way. . . . Problems which themselves contain clues as to how they should be solved would not test application. (p. 125)

As such, transferable performance tasks require students to address novel problems within and across new situations or contexts. In Hattie and Donoghue's (2016) study, "Learning Strategies: A Synthesis and Conceptual Model," transfer learning is most effectively addressed when students do the following:

❋ Solve problems in new situations (ES .80)

❋ See patterns in new situations (ES 1.14)

❋ Evaluate similarities and differences across contexts (ES 1.32)

What does this mean for teachers? It implies that as we choose or design transfer performance tasks, we must require students to analyze, evaluate, and solve problems in multiple contexts. This can be accomplished in a number of ways. Two methods are presented here.

The first method is a minor adaptation to currently recommended PBL design procedures. Teachers design an entry event that includes a transfer task with one context. Students work to solve that problem through the various phases of the project. At the conclusion of the project, students then encounter a new problem and spend time evaluating the problem with others (see Figure 2.2).

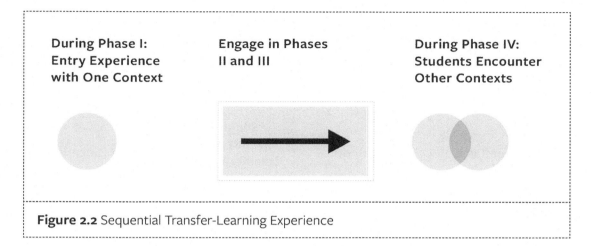

Figure 2.2 Sequential Transfer-Learning Experience

The second method is a significant shift from other forms of PBL design procedures. It starts students off with encountering multiple problem contexts (see Figure 2.3). In this approach, students must initially evaluate multiple contexts and identify the overarching problems that connect the contexts. From here, students may work on solving one of the contextualized problems. At the conclusion of the project, students are tasked with considering a novel problem or change in the current problem via a curveball or sequel.

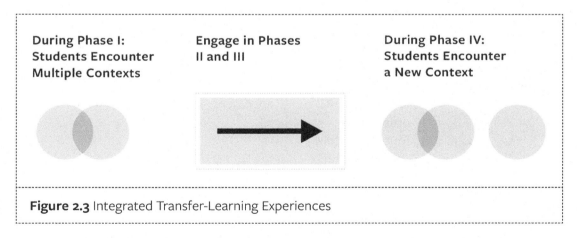

Figure 2.3 Integrated Transfer-Learning Experiences

There are multiple ways to design transfer tasks, including GRASPS, matrix problems, Four Act Tasks, and Gap Analysis (see Table 2.13). For an example of each, please see the online Appendix. These tasks were selected because they are straightforward to introduce and repeat in multiple projects. Our hope is that they are doable, and can grow habitual, as teachers and students learn together throughout the year. A more detailed explanation of GRASPS tasks and matrix problems are provided in Chapter 3, which discusses Phase 1 of a rigorous PBL unit.

Transfer Tasks	Description	Sequential or Integrated Transfer-Learning Experience	Text Location
GRASPS	A structured framework for defining problems within one or more contexts	In either a sequential or integrated approach	Chapter 3
Matrix Problems	A task that presents multiple unstructured problem contexts in which students identify commonalities to define and solve a shared problem across contexts	In an integrated approach	Chapter 3
Four Act Tasks	A linear approach to solving problems in four phases that resembles the hero's journey	In a sequential approach	Online Appendix

Transfer Tasks	Description	Sequential or Integrated Transfer-Learning Experience	Text Location
Gap Analysis	An approach that begins with a discrepancy between an ideal state and a current state; students work to mitigate the gap	In a sequential approach	Online Appendix

Table 2.13 Transfer Task Examples

Success Criteria: *Design transfer experiences, including entry events, curveballs, and sequels, for students to encounter at the transfer level of learning*

Once designing transfer tasks becomes second nature, planning for entry events, curveballs, and sequels is an easy fit. For example, when incorporated as part of the hook at the beginning, matrices may be woven into an entry event to pique students' questions and also introduce transfer early on. Curveballs and sequels tend to come at the end of a project, and they give students an opportunity to apply to a slightly changed context—or even a completely new one. GRASPS is one technique that might be used in sequels, which are discussed below.

Entry Events

Most problem- and project-based learning pedagogies include entry experiences or entry events. At the beginning of a project, these entry experiences or entry events place students in a scenario in which they need to solve a problem. After reviewing the transfer tasks you developed, select one to use for the launch of the project. On the project template, jot the down the following notes to remember before you launch:

❋ **Scenario:** What is the context or contexts you will introduce to students?

❊ **Expectations:** What is the major transfer task you will expect of them?

❊ **Patron:** Who will they be doing this task for? Who will students engage with throughout the project?

❊ **Format:** How will they show their work to you/others?

For more information
The online Appendix offers a wide variety of entry event experiences for you to consider. In addition, the next chapter walks through implementing an entry event experience in the classroom. If you want further information beyond this book, we encourage you to consider reviewing the *Rigorous PBL by Design Foundations Workbook* (McDowell, 2021a) for activities associated with developing and implementing entry event experiences.

Curveballs and Sequels

Rarely does life play by the rules. In baseball, a predictable steal at third base takes a turn when the runner gets caught in a rundown, or "pickle," between the two basemen. In a pandemic, teachers who expected to teach a room full of students must switch to remote instruction. Twists and turns are the norm rather than the exception. A core design habit for Rigorous PBL by Design is considering in advance how dynamics could change in the situation. Teachers should preplan for incorporating one of the following four changes for students. The following changes may be used for the whole class or may be offered to different students or groups of students throughout the final phase of the project.

Type of Curveball	Description	Example
Task Expectations	The product or the presentation students are working on has new specifications.	Instead of a written argument, the audience now requests a podcast.

Type of Curveball	Description	Example
Perspective Change	The students are tasked with understanding multiple perspectives within a problem context and how to incorporate those perspectives into the problem-based situation.	Instead of evaluating the perspective of anti-abortion voters, students understand the diverse perspectives of pro-choice and undecided voters.
Situational Change	Students face a change in the conditions of the context they are working in and must identify what and how they must change their understanding of the problem—and potentially their solution to the problem.	As students are working on an engineering problem, they learn that a specific component they need is delayed or unavailable for a number of months. They must look for alternatives, switch to another product, and adjust their timelines with vendors.
Cross-Context Problem	Students are faced with working on a new problem in a different context and are tasked with identifying what they can apply from their earlier problem to this new situation.	Students are working on an argumentative essay regarding the promotion or denial of universal transitional kindergarten and the funding offered by the government. They receive word that the nonprofit requesting these essays needs to change to a more pressing matter at hand: open-carry gun laws in restaurants and shops.

Table 2.14 Curveball Examples

Sequels are a type of curveball whereby students are expected to encourage a change after the project has concluded.

Habit 4: **Lock it (the schedule) in** *by setting tentative dates for workshops aligned to complexity levels*

We need to create a schedule to ensure that we meet the surface, deep, and transfer expectations within the confines of a school calendar. For teachers reading this book who are only looking to bring in a few transfer habits within their current sequence of lessons, the first success criteria provides different ways to sequence the instruction. It draws from our foundations in rigorous PBL, in which units start and end with transfer. The second success criteria, for teachers looking to design entire PBL units, explains how to calendar that approach.

Success Criteria: *Determine the sequence for meeting transfer, deep, and surface outcomes*

While working through the habits of this book, teachers may find there are times that another sequence outside of a problem-based sequence makes sense. Figure 2.4 illustrates a number of pathways to consider when designing units of study. Factors that might influence choosing one sequence over another include student pre-assessment data, content being learned, and the type of question that teachers may want to introduce first in the learning sequence.

Pathways of sequencing surface, deep, and transfer.

Pathway	Phase 1: Entry Point	Phase 2: Connecting	Phase 3: Integrating
Traditional	Surface	Surface ⟷ Deep	Surface Deep Transfer
Conceptual	Deep	Surface ⟷ Deep - - - - - - - - Deep ⟷ Transfer	Deep Transfer Surface
Problem/Project Based	Transfer	Deep ⟷ Transfer - - - - - - - - Transfer ⟷ Surface	Transfer Surface Deep

Levels of complexity and importance of all levels in learning.

Level 1: Isolation I have developed my understanding or skill in one of the key levels of learning.	**Level 2: Connection** I have connected my understanding or skill in two of the key levels of learning.	**Level 3: Integration** I have integrated my understanding or skill in all three levels of learning.
Surface o—o Deep o—o Transfer	Surface ⟷ Deep - - - - - - - - Deep ⟷ Transfer - - - - - - - - Transfer ⟷ Surface	Surface Deep Transfer - - - - - - - - Deep Transfer Surface - - - - - - - - Transfer Surface Deep

Figure 2.4 Complex Pathways
Source: Used with permission; McDowell, 2020.

Success Criteria: *Arrange and schedule workshops to meet surface, deep, and transfer outcomes on tentative dates*

Mapping out a calendar for implementing each phase is helpful in scheduling the four phases of the project. Simultaneously, a calendar is helpful to map out when you will begin a new habit and where you will follow through on that habit throughout the unit (see Table 2.15).

	Monday	Tuesday	Wednesday	Thursday	Friday
Week 1	Project Launch	Pre-assessment & discussion Review next steps	Surface workshop (jigsaw day 1)	Surface workshop (jigsaw day 2)	Surface workshop (direct instruction) Review next steps
Week 2	Surface workshop (read & annotate) Formative assessment Review next steps	Reteach surface as needed	Deep workshop (research guest panelist and write questions)	Deep workshop (interview guest panelist and debrief) Review next steps	Deep workshop (research and prepare for Socratic seminar)
Week 3	Deep workshop (feedback protocol for Socratic seminar questions & notes) Review next steps	Deep workshop (Socratic seminar)	Deep workshop (written reflection on current understanding)	Deep workshop (feedback protocol on written reflections, apply feedback) Review next steps	Assessment

	Monday	Tuesday	Wednesday	Thursday	Friday
Week 4	Discussion of assessment results and reteach Review next steps	Transfer Develop solutions, Review next steps	Transfer Students present solutions	Curveball Change in context— how do solutions change?	Reflection on learning

Table 2.15 Template and Sample Calendar
Note: See online Appendix for a detailed calendar example.

Success Criteria: *Use an easy-to-use template for organizing the design elements*

Template

The following template (see Table 2.16) is an offering for constructing rigorous PBL units. The steps in this chapter walk through each section of the unit plan. Check out the online Appendix for more Rigorous PBL by Design projects to use as models for designing your project.

Rigorous PBL by Design Project Planning Template

Learning Intentions	Learning Intentions	Learning Intentions	Learning Intentions
•	•	•	•

Success Criteria

Surface *Students will...* •	**Surface** *Students will...* •	**Surface** *Students will...* •	**Surface** *Students will...* •
Deep *Students will...* •	**Deep** *Students will...* •	**Deep** *Students will...* •	**Deep** *Students will...* •

Transfer Success Criteria

Students will...
•

Contexts
Include potential patrons, audience, or purpose

Questions

Surface	Deep	Transfer (Driving Questions)
•	•	•

Tasks

Surface	Deep	Transfer (Products, Performances, Portfolios)
Students will... •	*Students will...* •	*Students will...* •
		Design Curveballs/Sequels

Workshops		
Surface	**Deep**	**Transfer**
•	•	•
Calendar		
How will you launch transfer-level work with students? (Narrative)		

Table 2.16 Rigorous PBL by Design Template

💡 Conclusion

The template process enables teachers to set up a plan for engaging in Rigorous PBL by Design. The template should be thought of as a rough draft, constantly being altered and changed as the project is implemented. Those augmentations occur because of what teachers learn from classroom interactions. Ultimately, the habits of this chapter do not directly lead to an impact on students—but they can be a support mechanism for the in-action habits that are discussed throughout the remainder of the book.

❓ Review Questions

❋   To what extent do the design habits in this chapter reflect what you already do when you are designing new units of study?

☛   How do you currently "make it clear" with students? What actions do you take to ensure students are clear? What actions do students take to ensure they are clear on expectations?

☛   How do you currently ensure students "see it (the learning) everywhere"? After reviewing the success criteria, what are next steps to ensure students are engaging in transfer learning and have a level of voice and choice in doing so?

☛   To what extent are you "planning for the right fit" with tasks that align to surface, deep, and transfer learning? What are potential next steps for you in this area?

☛   How are you "locking in" the schedule to make sure students are learning surface, deep, and transfer outcomes? What is the next step in your planning to ensure everything fits in your schedule?

❋   What are key similarities and differences between your design process for deep and transfer learning and the recommendations here?

❋   What is your current experience with integrating a transfer task at the beginning of a unit?

❋   How do the templates offered here and in the online Appendix align with your current unit design? What are the key differences? What inferences do you draw about how these differences influence teacher and student habits in the classroom?

✳   How can you build a unit and prepare for adjustments along the way? Who do you trust to give you meaningful feedback before, during, and after the project?

Next Steps

✳   Build a draft project unit using one of the templates.

✳   Receive feedback from colleagues using the Tuning protocol (included in the online Appendix).

✳   Set a date for implementing this project and ask a colleague to observe the launch.

✳   Celebrate the start!

Chapter 3

PHASE 1: PROJECT LAUNCH

> **"**
>
> Ya got trouble, folks
> Right here in River City,
> trouble with a capital *T*
>
> —Robert Preston

In the Broadway musical *The Music Man,* the title character warns the people of an Iowa town against a problem they didn't see coming. "Ya got trouble folks," goes the popular song. "Right here in River City." His portentous tune rallies the townspeople to meet a challenge: How can they maintain the wholesome values of River City as modernization threatens to sully the morals of their young people? Projects, at their best, begin this way too. From the very start, students are met with a challenge (or challenges) that they must face.

The first phase of Rigorous PBL by Design, where students meet their challenge, is called the project launch. As the name suggests, its purpose is not just to start a new unit of learning but to launch learners into a trajectory wherein they will learn, grow, and work together to address a driving question. There is trouble in River City, and it is up to our students to find a solution.

Phase 1 is a critical part of the project-based learning process because it

❋ sets the tone for a culture of shared work,

❋ establishes clarity of the problem or problems,

❋ builds a set of questions and facts students need to learn (or "need to know") to meet the challenges, and

❋ begins with transfer-level teaching and learning strategies.

Three habits are key to making the project launch doable in classrooms (see Table 3.1). This chapter unpacks each one, revealing why it is crucial to implementing this first phase of rigorous PBL.

Rigorous PBL Teacher Habit	Success Criteria
Habit 5: **Start with a challenge** by setting your purpose with an entry event and getting students clear on what they're learning and what success looks like	~ Launch transfer-level expectations with a purposeful entry experience for all ~ Crystalize learning intentions, success criteria, and the driving question with students
Habit 6: **Name the gaps** by pre-assessing and discussing the results with students	~ Conduct a pre-assessment ~ Facilitate a discussion with students on their performance and next steps they can take via a protocol (ongoing criteria throughout the project)
Habit 7: **Look ahead** by creating next steps based on knows/need-to-knows and holding to learning agreements and protocols	~ Facilitate the know/need-to-know list and create next steps ~ Hold to agreements and protocols that maximize the learning zone

Table 3.1 Project Launch Habits

Habit 5: **Start with a challenge** *by setting your purpose with an entry event and getting students clear on what they're learning and what success looks like*

On the first day of the unit, students must face their own "trouble in River City" moment. Seasoned practitioners of PBL will recognize this as an entry experience or entry event. Entry events are meant to provide challenging work up front so that a shared reason for learning can drive the work forward. Moreover, this introduces transfer-level expectations to students from the start.

Providing challenging work up front also requires clarifying the learning intentions and success criteria for students. Clear expectations are essential for students to know where they are going and where they stand in relation to that goal. Success criteria will be divided into surface, deep, and transfer levels so that a clear path for learning is created with students.

Success Criteria: *Launch transfer-level expectations with a purposeful entry experience for all*

In an entry experience, teachers ask students to work through a series of questions such as:

✳ What do you think we are going to solve?

✳ What content standards do we need to learn? Why do we need to learn this information?

✳ What will we be designing, creating, or producing? For whom?

✳ How will success criteria look at surface, deep, and transfer levels?

✳ What do we know? What do we need to know?

An entry event will help students answer the questions listed above. The range of entry events that might launch students into learning are limited only by your imagination. Remember—if entry events are to be part of a habit we frequently turn to, they should be as simple as possible.

Teachers may start with entry events that mirror those in traditional project-based learning. In that case, trouble still awaits in River City. However, teachers may choose to expand by introducing students to multiple contexts at once. To extend our metaphor, there is trouble in River City, as well as Metropolis and Narnia too. When we understand the root cause, we may even find that there is trouble next door. Both approaches are discussed below.

Single Context

Entry events that introduce a single, real-world context can take many forms. They may be text based, for example, such as news articles, journal readings, or letters. They may also rely on visuals, such as videos, photographs, or a collection of artwork. Entry events can even be interactive and immersive, utilizing real-time interviews or a nature walk.

Scan the QR codes in Table 3.2 to see the examples of various entry events in the online Appendix.

Videos	Artwork	Letter
Driving Question: How can we deepen our understanding when we ask better *wh-* questions? (ELD)	Driving Question: How should we tell the story of American progress? (U.S. History)	Driving Question: Which additional strategies should I use to solve problems? (Grade 1 Math)

Table 3.2 Entry Event Examples

Multiple Contexts and Co-Construction

Traditionally, Day 1 presents students with a problem to solve. But what if, instead of a ready-made problem, students encounter a set of complex situations? Rarely are innovators outside of school presented with a clearly defined question to answer. More often, the first real task of a problem-solver is to scan a complex situation and articulate the best question to be asking in the first place.

Take the challenge of relocating a farmers' market, for instance: Local growers need to increase the number of buyers in the community so that their food stands are profitable. County regulations require a space that has a clear point of entry and exit, rather than an open park. Food vendors have requested better access to electricity and wide roads to haul in their equipment. And during the month of January, the city needs extra square footage reserved to make room for an outdoor ice-skating rink. Before the manager of the farmers' market can propose a solution, she must ask the right question. Where could the market operate in a way that improves access to farmers, vendors, and families while still meeting municipal regulations?

Most problem-solving processes prescribed in business literature begin with a common step: define the problem. The saying goes, "If I were given an hour to save the planet, I would spend 59 minutes defining the problem and 1 minute resolving it." In following this pattern with students, we present them with challenging work up front. We also give them a purpose for analyzing patterns across situations—and that's teaching to transfer at day 1!

Let's take a deep dive into two transfer-level tasks that involve multiple contexts and co-construction and can be used at the beginning of a project.

GRASPS Framework and Authentic Situations

In 2021, McTighe presented his work on the GRASPS framework as a means for creating criteria for performance-based assessments (see Figure 3.1). These criteria include

* a real-world goal,

* a meaningful role for the students,

* an authentic (or simulated) audience,

* a contextualized situation that involves real-world application,

* student-generated culminating products and/or performances, and

* success criteria by which student products and performances will be evaluated as evidence of learning.

Goal

- Your task is to ....
- The goal is to ....
- The problem/challenge is ....
- The obstacle(s) to overcome is (are) ....

Role

- You are ....
- You have been asked to ....
- Your job is to..

Audience

- Your client(s) is (are) ....
- The target audience ....
- You need to convince ....

Situation

- The context you find yourself in is ....
- The challenge involves dealing with ....

Product/Performance and Purpose

- You will create a ....
  in order to ....
- You need to develop ....
  so that ....

Standards and Criteria for Success

- Your performance needs ....
- Your work will be judged by ....
- Your product must meet the following standards ....
- A successful result will ....

Figure 3.1 GRASPS Scaffold
Source: McTighe & Gareis, 2021.

GRASPS Prompts	Authentic Situation Example 1
Goal	

~ Your task is to:
~ The goal is to:
~ The problem/
  challenge is:
~ The obstacle(s) to over-
  come is (are):
	~ Examine the percentage of plastics in the local waterways
	~ Report to local community council members on your learning and rec-
	  ommendations for future action
	~ That reports reveal that plastics have emerged within drinking water
	~ Identifying the percentage of plastics in local drinking water, as well as
	  determining the source, density, and distribution; who is impacted; and
	  what recommendations you have for the town council

Role	
~ You are: ~ You have been asked to: ~ Your job is to:	~ Student advisers at a local college ~ Work on a project on behalf of a nearby community ~ Provide a presentation, executive summary, and list of recommendations
Situation	

~ The context you find
  yourself in is:
~ The job involves
  dealing with:
	~ Evaluating local waterways for a community council
	~ Measurements of water quality, interviews with community members,
	  and engagement with local municipality organizations and council mem-
	  bers

Presentation	

~ You will create a:
~ In order to:
~ You need to develop:
~ So that:
	~ Presentation and executive summary
	~ Provide recommendations to a council
	~ A frame of presenting the problem, solution criteria, possible solutions,
	  recommended solutions, and a plan for implementation and inspection
	~ You can explain how the water pollution problem can be mitigated or
	  eliminated

Standards and Criteria for Success	

~ Your performance
  needs to:
~ Your work will be
  judged by:
~ Your product must meet
  the following standards:
~ A successful result will:
	~ Account for three standards—design a solution to a real-world problem
	  based on student-generated evidence (ESS3); write an argument, sup-
	  ported by relevant sources (W1); and present on a topic (SL4).
	~ Council members along with local community members and public
	  organizations you worked with
	~ five-to-seven-minute presentation, and two-to-three-page executive
	  summary
	~ Meet the task and content success criteria and receive reasonable
	  approval from stakeholder groups

Table 3.3 GRASPS Scenario Example

If teachers choose a sequential approach to their project, then students engage with GRASPS at the beginning and the end. (You know you're thinking it: a GRASPS sandwich.) At the project start, students face their first GRASPS scenario. At the conclusion of the project, students then face a new GRASPS scenario and compare and contrast that scenario with the one they faced earlier in the project.

In an integrated approach, students engage with multiple GRASPS scenarios up front, identify the key themes across all the challenges, and select one of the scenarios to work on in a small group (see Table 3.3). Another option would be that student groups may be working on different GRASPS scenarios in the same classroom. For instance, one group may be working on the plastics problem while another group is looking at insurance premiums in California. While the contexts are different, the surface- and deep-level knowledge and skills students need to learn regarding each are identical for all scenarios. This allows teachers to provide similar instructional support to all students during Phases 1, 2, and 3 and diversify instruction during Phase 4.

Matrix Problems

Matrix problems are designed to give students multiple scenarios up front in the learning process and provide them with the opportunity to determine the underlying driving questions and learning outcomes. Matrices require presenting two or more contexts to students, using a protocol to help students generate a series of questions and discern the overall learning outcome, and a means for writing down and discussing their thinking (such as a Venn diagram).

Table 3.4 illustrates two primary examples and Table 3.5 a secondary example of a matrix problem, along with a Venn diagram for four contexts.

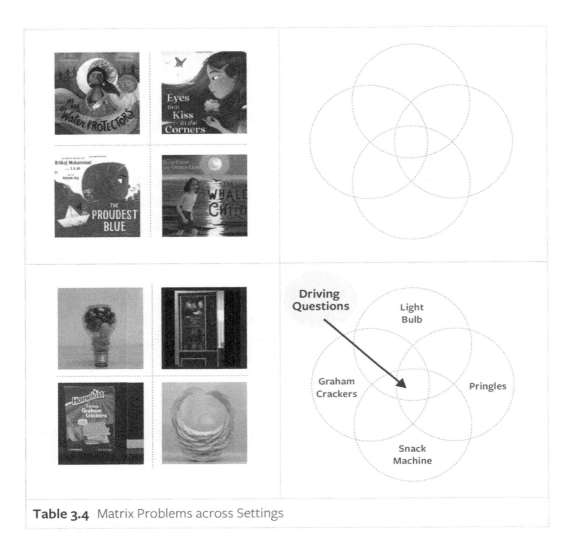

Table 3.4 Matrix Problems across Settings

Matrices are an ideal way to engage in project launches. They are easy to replicate and employ the power of visuals to quickly present multiple situations to students. In Table 3.4, one example is asking students to compare contexts through stories (see detailed information on this unit in Table 3.6). The other is comparing different contexts related to counting.

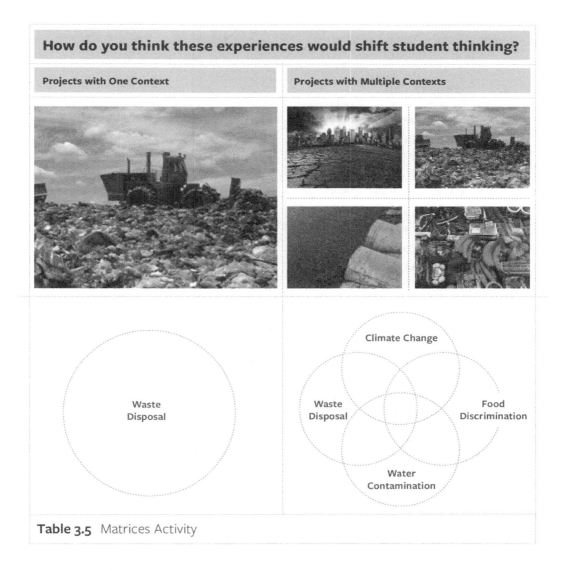

Table 3.5 Matrices Activity

Student interactions with matrices can be structured in various ways. A jigsaw is one useful strategy to employ so that expert groups of students can familiarize themselves with one context at a time and share their learning with peers. For classes that need to remain whole group, interactive presentation tools such as Pear Deck and Nearpod are useful to solicit individual contributions and promote class-wide discussion. Table 3.6 illustrates an elementary (second grade) example and a high school (ninth grade) example. The jigsaw protocol can be found in the online Appendix.

Second-Grade Project Literacy and Social Studies		Ninth-Grade Project Biology and Social Studies	
Project Title: *Building Better Communities*		**Project Title:** *Don't Drink the Water*	
Learning Intentions: Students will . . . ~ Integrate important facts to present the central message, lesson, or moral of several stories (California Common Core Standard RL 2.2, RL 2.7) ~ Compare and contrast the similarities and differences between people in their own community and other communities (Next Generation Social Studies Framework 2.2)		Learning Intentions. Students will . . . ~ Formulate solutions to sustain biodiversity in and across ecosystems (Next Generation Science Standards LS4.D, HS-LS4-5, HS-LS4-5) ~ Evaluate and take and defend positions on the scope and limits of rights and obligations as democratic citizens, the relationships among them, and how they are secured (California State Standard HSS 12.2)	

Success Criteria			
Goal 1: Present the central message of several stories.		**Goal 2: Compare and contrast similarities and differences between people in my own community and other communities.**	
Surface	**Deep**	**Surface**	**Deep**
~ Define central message ~ Describe the who, what, when, where, and why of a story ~ Identify important facts about characters and settings	~ Connect what you know about the character and settings to the central message of the story	~ *Define unique, culture, values, and community* ~ List physical and cultural features about myself ~ List physical and cultural features about others	~ Identify similarities and differences between people in my community and other communities

Transfer
Present a response to literature that connects the messages in multiple texts to life in my community.

Table 3.6 Matrix Entry Events in Primary and Secondary Environments (continued)

Success Criteria			
Goal 1:		**Goal 2:**	
🌷 **Surface**	🌷 **Deep**	🌷 **Surface**	🌷 **Deep**
~ Match criteria for developing a solution including costs, safety, reliability, and aesthetic as related to social, cultural, and environmental impacts ~ List different ways to convey problems and solutions ~ Define trade-offs using qualitative and quantitative methods ~ Describe the importance of involving multiple experts in different fields to solve problems ~ Explain what it means to evaluate the impact and viability of new technologies on society and the environment ~ Give examples of mitigation, cost analysis, environmental impact, risks, and benefits	~ Analyze problem-solving methods and determine the best for various contexts ~ Evaluate previous decisions based on process, trade-offs, and mitigation considerations ~ Interpret the effectiveness of bringing in multiple perspectives to make a decision ~ Draw conclusions about trade-offs using qualitative and quantitative data to determine potential solutions that consider costs, safety, and reliability	~ Discuss the meaning of the rights to freedom of religion, speech, press, assembly, petition, and privacy ~ Explain the importance of economic rights to the individual and to society, including the right to acquire, use, transfer, and dispose of property, and the right to protect one's work through copyrights and patents, and right to be represented by unions. ~ Describe the obligations of civic-mindedness, including voting, being informed on civic issues, and entering into public service, the military, or an alternative service ~ Give examples of the principle of reciprocity between rights and obligations	~ Assess the effectiveness of the government in protecting the rights guaranteed under the Bill of Rights ~ Compare and contrast economic rights to individual and societal demands ~ Cite supporting evidence for the principle of reciprocity between rights and obligations ~ Explain connections among obligations, rights of individual citizens, and the Bill of Rights

Transfer

~ Formulate a solution to a real-world problem that involves multiple contexts.
~ Create and present a decision related to a real-world problem.
~ Evaluate the implementation of a solution from one context to another context.

Table 3.6 Matrix Entry Events in Primary and Secondary Environments (continued)

Example Entry Event	Example Entry Event
The covers of four books representing diverse cultures are placed on chart paper around the room for a gallery walk. Students walk to each chart paper and make predictions—what do they notice? What do they predict this story will be about?	Students will develop the driving question, co-construct success criteria and evaluate their list against the one developed by the teacher(s), create next steps, and develop benchmarks to meet expectations along the way.
Students join their table groups, and each table is given a map representing one of the book covers they just viewed and a short video to watch about the region.	The teacher will start the transfer-level work by having students engage in a jigsaw activity. Students will get into groups of four, and each group will review a number of articles and videos on one of four scenarios. Once students have reviewed the material, they will discuss with one another what they learned using a Final Word protocol.
Once table groups have watched their short video, examined their map, and reviewed the predictions on chart paper about their book cover, they share their findings with the whole class via Whip Around protocol.	
Next, students work in small groups or individually to brainstorm the driving question on paper (with a teacher-provided sentence stem). Teacher follows up with a whole-class discussion to develop the driving question.	Next, the teacher will reassign students to new groups that include one person to represent each scenario. The students will then discuss the similarities and differences between the scenarios. The students will then head back to their original groups and engage in a Carousel Brainstorm (a specific protocol for generating questions and responding to prompts), drafting a range of questions along the surface-, deep-, and transfer-level continuum. Next, students will select a driving question and potential success criteria to meet those outcomes.
After developing the driving question, the teacher presents students with the two primary learning intentions. Students circle words that are important or new to them and use those to construct surface success criteria. Teacher uses prompts such as "more than one" and "comparing" to help co-construct deep and transfer success criteria.	

Table 3.6 Matrix Entry Events in Primary and Secondary Environments (continued). **Note:** This project could be completed in one discipline rather than the two subjects shown in the examples above.

The suggestion here is to expand the way you launch rigorous PBL projects by presenting students with multiple contexts. Rather than your giving students a driving question, students are asked to create their own driving question and suggest their own products to create and present.

Using GRASPS or matrices, or any of the aforementioned transfer tasks, is a way to help get teachers and students unstuck in their thinking about what they are learning. Our aim is to ask them, habitually, where else their learning applies in situations beyond a single context.

One important note here is that when students are invited to co-construct a driving question, be prepared to shift. A driving question developed in isolation from students may or may not align with students' interests or their own generation of the question. We want to make sure that we are not holding on to a question that is irrelevant to students or maybe less engaging than we originally assumed. In his article "The Code for Student Engagement," Chad Prather (2021), a coach in Metro Nashville Public Schools, writes about how he augmented his question to connect to students' current reality rather than using a question that was either in the past or future or too theoretical for students to connect with. In addition, he shares that all students come with prior experiences and knowledge. Not all of their prior knowledge, however, relates to the core content we are trying to teach. As such, we need to take a formative mindset to our questions and be prepared to change our driving questions at the beginning of, and sometimes throughout, the unit. To paraphrase J. R. R. Tolkien, there is no one question to rule them all. Questions should be evolving and co-constructed.

Success Criteria: *Crystalize learning intentions and success criteria with students*

One habit we may need to relinquish from our repertoire is giving students our expectations of learning outright. Yes, we want them to be clear. Clarity has a high likelihood of significantly improving learning, and it's the lynchpin to factors such as feedback and assessment-capable learners. And yes, we want learning intentions and success criteria. Moreover, we want them to matter to students. But if our habit is to dictate expectations of learning every time, we might find ourselves holding a tight grip on a schema in which the teacher holds all the power.

Rubrics remain a clear, holistic way to clarify expectations—but they mean more when students have already engaged in a productive struggle with material. Entry events that include work samples, or simply analyzing work samples early in the project, present an opportunity to engage in conversation about expectations, rather than simply presenting them to students.

Habit 1, presenting challenging material up front, aims to develop clarity while integrating deep- and transfer-level learning strategies. A core tenet of this practice is that students see high-quality, or transfer-level, exemplars early in the project sequence. One of the most effective ways to do this is to use exemplars as part of the co-construction process.

One classic way to co-construct success criteria is evaluating examples. In this strategy, students receive two or three work samples of varying quality and are asked to work in small groups to rank them from strongest to weakest. Following this ranking, students list or circle what sets the different samples apart from one another. Lastly, the teacher facilitates a discussion with the class in which they identify success criteria for the work at hand. The co-constructed success criteria can then be recorded on a bulletin board, note cards in student folders, or digital documents. These success criteria then become a touchstone for peer feedback, lesson objectives, and assessments.

Clarity comes best through conversation, not presentation. This is why we advocate for co-constructing learning intentions and success criteria with students. Co-construction is a process by which teachers and students work together to identify the expectations of learning or the driving question. Researcher Shirley Clarke (2021) notes that co-construction often results in increased student confidence and self-efficacy, as well as improved abilities to self- and peer assess.

A number of other strategies may be utilized to help students co-construct with their teacher. In Table 3.7, you'll find seven strategies of co-construction that may be used across elementary and high school contexts.

Co-Construction Title	Description
Multiple Contexts	Students will . . . ~ evaluate two or more situations that relate to the learning intention and success criteria of the problem or project; ~ generate potential learning intentions and success criteria along with potential questions that they may solve during the project (via a jigsaw protocol); ~ receive the teacher's learning intention and success criteria and determine the similarities and differences between the teacher's and the student's work; and ~ generate what they know, what they need to know, and next steps to address the driving question.
Clues Approach	Students will . . . ~ review the learning intention and a set of verbs for surface-, deep-, and transfer-level outcomes; ~ work in small groups to populate the success criteria by matching the verbs with student-constructed criteria; ~ attempt to develop consensus on student-constructed success criteria; ~ receive the teacher's learning intention and success criteria and determine the similarities and differences between the teacher's and the student's work; and ~ generate what they know, what they need to know, and next steps to address the driving question.

Co-Construction Title	Description
Silent Protocol	Students will . . . ~ observe teachers demonstrating a successful example or successful process without talking; ~ write down the specific steps they think teachers are taking to demonstrate success; ~ review their specific steps with others and attempt to form consensus; ~ observe teachers demonstrating a successful example or successful process without talking again and then refine their steps; ~ compare and contrast the teacher's learning intention and success criteria and determine the similarities and differences between the teacher's and the student's work; and ~ generate what they know, what they need to know, and next steps to address the driving question.
Evaluating Examples	Students will . . . ~ review one or more examples of the applied learning intention; ~ determine the learning intention and success criteria; ~ review their specific criteria with others and attempt to form consensus; ~ receive the teacher's learning intention and success criteria and determine the similarities and differences between the teacher's and the student's work; ~ rank exemplars based on the teacher's criteria; and ~ generate what they know, what they need to know, and next steps to address the driving question.

Co-Construction Title	Description
Reconstructing Assessments	Students will . . . ~ evaluate assessment questions and rank them against leveled success criteria verbs; ~ determine the learning intentions and success criteria; ~ compare and contrast the teacher's learning intention and success criteria and determine the similarities and differences between the teacher's and the student's work; ~ generate a number of driving questions and potential contexts at the transfer level of learning; and ~ generate what they know, what they need to know, and next steps to address the driving question.
Student Drafting	Students will . . . ~ review the learning intention and brainstorm success criteria; ~ incorporate teacher-generated success criteria into their list; ~ review exemplars and add or modify current success criteria; ~ organize success criteria into leveled success criteria (i.e., surface, deep, and transfer); ~ evaluate exemplars and refine their success criteria with peers and the teacher; and ~ generate what they know, what they need to know, and next steps to address the driving question.
Error Analysis	Students will . . . ~ detect errors in a text (or other medium) or via teacher modeling, ~ present specific criteria to be considered to correct the error, ~ write down success criteria, ~ generate the learning intention, and ~ practice using the success criteria and giving and receiving feedback.

Table 3.7 Co-Construction Strategies
Note: Examples of each co-construction strategy can be found in the online Appendix.

Habit 6: **Name the gaps** *by pre-assessing and discussing the results with students*

There is likely no learning factor at the student level that is more powerful than assessment-capable learners (Hattie, 2009). When a student knows the expectations of learning, how it relates to their current performance, and what next steps they need to take to improve, they are learning how to learn. Teachers can create conditions that position students for assessment capability every time they launch a project. The entry event and co-construction experience are practices that orient students to what they need to learn. A pre-assessment, paired with discussion, can show the students—and their teacher—just how far they have to go. It creates fertile ground for assessment-capable learning to take root.

Success Criteria: *Conduct a pre-assessment*

When creating a pre-assessment, keep in mind who the assessment is for: the students. The purpose of a pre-assessment is to help learners understand where they are in relation to the learning goals, not to exhaust their efforts or create more grading for the teacher. In other words, keep it brief. A quick (10-question) assessment that spans surface, deep, and transfer expectations should be sufficient to orient learners. Surface questions may include listing, defining, matching, or labeling information. Deep questions should be based on short-response questions related to the general principles of the discipline or disciplines they are going to study. Transfer questions should center on application-based, short-response questions.

Graham Nuthall's research found that students already knew, on average, about 50% of what teachers wanted them to learn *before* instruction began (2007). Not surprisingly, his research also indicated that knowledge was distributed unevenly throughout different groups of students. Different students arrive at school harboring different background knowledge. In Nuthall's summation, only about 20% of students begin a unit study possessing little to no background knowledge. Identifying where any one student may sit on this spectrum, for every topic and unit of study, would be overwhelming for a teacher to gauge every time. But students can help bring that information to light, for the teachers and themselves, with a pre-assessment. Two examples of pre-assessment leveled at surface, deep, and transfer levels are given in Table 3.8 below.

Example 1:
English Language Development

Speaking Pre-Assessment—Vocab 1.1

I. Say each word aloud:

1. Could	2. Cherish	3. Persevere	4. Challenge
5. Activist	6. Thought	7. Goal	8. Exhausted

II. Use the vocabulary word in bold to address each prompt below:

1. Question: What do you **cherish**?
   Answer: I **cherish** _____.

2. Question: Describe something you never **thought** you **could** do but now can.
   Answer: I never **thought** I **could** _____, but now I can.

3. Question: Describe someone who has **persevered** in the face of **challenges**.
   Answer: _____ has **persevered** in the face of **challenges**.

4. Question: Describe a time when you are **exhausted**.
   Answer: I am **exhausted** after I _____.

III. Use FOUR vocabulary words in sentences that discuss the story *Fauja Singh Keeps Going*.

_____

Table 3.8 Pre-Assessment Examples

Example 2: Math

Unit 4 Pre-Assessment

Success Criteria: I can...	Problem	Got it?
...follow a pattern to find the next terms.	Term 1 Term 2 Term 3 1 2 3 ☐ 00 0000 000000 ☐ ☐	
...recall the formula for slope intercept form.	Write it here:	
...complete an input table. ...graph a line based on a table. ...describe the slope on a line graph.	Term Number / Number of objects table: 1→3, 2→7, 3→11, 4→, 5→	
...calculate the rate of change.	Circle the correct answer, based on the table above: A) 3 B) 1 C) 7 D) 4	
...write an equation based on a table.	Write it here; use the table above:	
...predict the value for the 20th term.	Write it here; use the equation above:	

Table 3.8 Pre-Assessment Examples, continued
Source: Adapted from Miller, 2019.

Alternatively, teachers may prefer to go even leaner in their pre-assessments. Classroom discussions can be just as useful as a pretest on paper to help students and teachers orient themselves to what's ahead. Here are a few ways to generate student data from the entire class:

❋ Give every student a whiteboard to write their answers and show the class.

❋ Provide all students with a set of note cards that have a 1, 2, 3, or 4, or A, B, C, or D, to show you and others their response to a multiple-choice question.

❋ Ask students to move to a corner of the classroom based on their response to a question. For instance, you give them a scenario that has two answers. Students move to one side of the classroom based on their answer.

Success Criteria: *Facilitate a discussion with students on their performance and next steps they can take via a protocol (ongoing criteria throughout the project)*

After giving pre-assessments, don't let the paint dry. As humans, we are inclined to seek protection and avoid vulnerability. It is a natural act to hide what we don't know. As teachers, when we capitulate to this urge, we can unwittingly perpetuate classroom cultures where the finished product is celebrated more than progress. Here, early in the project, is a chance to bring what is unknown to light.

The purpose of this early measure of understanding is to create dialogue with learners. Teachers play a vital role here to promote a classroom culture where it is safe to show what you don't know yet. After they've tried their hand with a pre-assessment, invite students to reflect on the following questions:

❋ What did you already know?

❋ What did you think you knew that was actually incorrect? Why do you think that is the case?

❋ Where were you close to getting a question right but missed a subtle detail?

❋ What do you need to know?

Admitting what you don't know can be unnerving at first. Teachers can help by modeling curiosity above ego and using routines that foster emotional safety. This, after all, is where all learners begin. Once this mindset takes hold, discussing pre-assessments becomes a doable habit. To support this habit in being accessible to students, teachers need to show interest in students' thinking (especially when that thinking is wrong). There are three simple ways to demonstrate interest in student thinking.

* **Ask questions:** Provide students with a number of questions to prompt thinking and to encourage their ideas. What makes you think that? What are you assuming? To what extent could you be incorrect? Why would other people pick this solution or another solution? How will you find out if you are correct?

* **Celebrate diversity of thought:** Share with students that you are absolutely fascinated by the amount of answers students have from a question and that you are interested in finding out how everyone will come to consensus on one answer over time.

* **Suspend judgment:** Don't tell them the right answer immediately. Allow students to discuss with each other the different answers and determine why people would select certain outcomes. After a workshop when the correct answer is presented, this is a good time to have students reflect on the change between the misconception and the correct answer.

Engage students in structured protocols to reflect on their current thinking. Since this step takes place before much instruction has occurred, their thinking is likely to include misconceptions and incomplete information, as well as completely accurate knowledge and skills. Structured protocols that support students in making sense of gaps or discrepancies include the following those recorded in Table 3.9.

Protocol Name	Source Found in Online Appendix
I Used to Think/Now I Think	Harvard Project Zero
What? So What? Now What?	School Reform Initiative
ESP+I	Cultures of Thinking
Gap Analysis	School Reform Initiative
PG&E	Predict-Gather-Explain
Be-Sure-To	Be-Sure-To

Table 3.9 Evaluating and Taking Action on Misconceptions

Additional strategies are available, including discussion mapping, which can be an excellent, low-prep strategy. Recording early on who is ready to share their thinking, and who isn't, can be a simple way to measure growth. Other protocols to structure the discussion include Fishbowl and Learning Dilemma (protocol resource banks are provided in the online Appendix, including Harvard's Project Zero, National School Reform Faculty website, and School Reform Initiative). This investment in routine will pay off throughout the project. Once students—and the teacher—are comfortable discussing their current status and next steps, this can be repeated in lock step with formative assessments along the way.

Habit 7: **Look ahead** *by creating next steps based on knows/need-to-knows and holding to learning agreements and protocols*

The conclusion of the project launch is designed to prepare for the more convergent, concrete phases of the project. This is a place where students consolidate what they know and need to know and review what is expected to solve the problem or problems presented to them at the beginning of the phase. This routine is initiated at the end of the project launch in a way that is careful and responsive to students. As the project continues, a habitual revisit of "Where are we now?" and "Where to next?" will help synthesize learning and jointly decide next steps.

Success Criteria: *Facilitate the know/need-to-know list and create next steps*

Once expectations are clear, and the class has discussed their pre-assessment, it's time to capture knows and need-to-knows on a class document. This document can live on chart paper, a bulletin board, or a digital slide. As a class, students will develop a T-chart that illustrates what they already know about the project, as well as key questions or need-to-knows. The foundation for this information comes from the previous set of activities and serves as a means for identifying next steps.

Teachers may want to use the following protocols to generate the K/NTK list or make decisions on core next steps:

＊ **Think-Pair-Share:** Give students time to generate a list of knows and need-to-knows on their own. Depending on their age, they may want to generate theirs using pictures or words. Students often benefit from a concrete number here. For example, five knows and five need-to-knows per person is a good place to start. After each student has their list, they share with a partner and may add to their own list, if they hear something new. Each pair offers one know and need-to-know for the class document, until all knows and need-to-knows have been captured.

✳ **Group Whip Around:** Each table or group of students generates its own know and need-to-know list. Again, if students need a concrete number of knows and need-to-knows here, give it to them. Once each group has their list, the teacher facilitates a Whip Around: each group is asked for one know or need-to-know at a time. The cycle continues until all knows and need-to-knows have been captured.

To co-construct next steps based on the knows/need-to-knows, the above protocols may be repeated with a new prompt: What do we do next? Or, to keep the time frame tidy, a teacher may also choose to quickly facilitate a next- steps discussion based on what the class needs to know.

> **Note for exceptional learners:** Independent processing time is essential here. If the class launches directly into knows and need-to-knows as a whole group, students who need extra time tend to remain silent while the rest of the class jumps into making a list. When students are given time to think and record on their own, and then give/get ideas from a partner or small group, they are better situated to contribute to the discussion. Students who are reluctant to speak will further benefit from a quiet heads-up. "I like what you have here. I am going to call on you second so we make sure to capture this on the board" can help prepare students to share with the class.

At this point, the metaphorical journey to save River City has begun. The problem has been identified, criteria for success are clear, and the class has collectively named what they know and still need to know. To keep a clear learning path at the forefront, teachers may elect to point out here that the class will transition to Phase 2 and will cover the surface-level knowledge first. If a teacher takes this stance, consider revisiting the K/NTK list to identify key surface-learning questions. One way to do this is to circle the surface-level questions (e.g., "What does X mean?") and explain that this is where the class will go first. An example of what this can look like in a K/NTK chart is provided in Table 3.10.

Leveled Know/Need-to-Know List

Line of Inquiry	Know	Need-to-Know
Surface · What? · How?		
Deep · Why?		
Transfer · Should? · When? · Where? · Why?		

Table 3.10 Leveled Know/Need-to-Know List

Once the class is familiar with the K/NTK process, revisit this routine frequently as a way to recap the day's learning. This habit of synthesizing will help return students' attention to the broader scope of the project. It's also smart teaching. We have a high degree of retention (memory) for whatever happens during the last portion of a learning block (Sousa, 2017). How often are those valuable sticky minutes spent on turning in papers or calling out homework reminders for the next day? While the genesis of the class K/NTK chart requires a deliberate analysis of the entry event and thoughtful protocols to include all learners, a habitual revisit can take five minutes or less. It can take the form of exit tickets, short reflections, or a quick discussion about the knows/need-to-knows. It is also a simple and smart way to ensure that learning sticks.

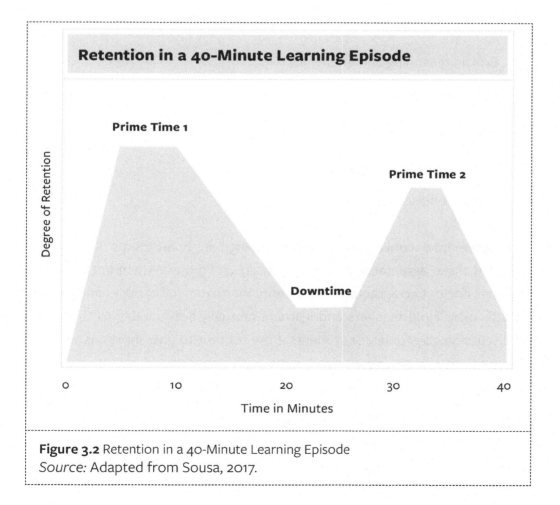

Figure 3.2 Retention in a 40-Minute Learning Episode
Source: Adapted from Sousa, 2017.

Success Criteria: *Hold to agreements and protocols that maximize the learning zone*

Agreements and protocols help "build the container" for staying in the learning zone. They help nudge teachers and students into a space of experimentation, play, and welcoming errors. Naming these norms together, and habitually making reference to them, is critical to making those agreements meaningful. While these agreements could be utilized anywhere and anytime in the project process, we mention them in the first phase of the project so that they might be ongoing. These agreements include:

* ❋ State views and ask genuine questions

* ❋ Share all relevant information

* ❋ Use specific examples and agree on what important words mean

* ❋ Explain reasoning and intent

* ❋ Focus on interests, not positions

* ❋ Test assumptions and inferences

* ❋ Jointly design next steps

* ❋ Discuss undiscussable issues

Imagine how conversations would change in boardrooms and grade-level meetings if these agreements were truly realized. Embrace them in the classroom. Sometimes one or two agreements are plenty for a room full of busy hands and minds, and that's okay. Hold teachers and learners mutually accountable to them. When a class discussion goes quiet, or students grow content to give short answers without explaining their reasons, agreements such as the ones above help us to remember that to learn is to push our thinking—and that's what we're here for.

Author Guy Claxton (2019) describes the learning zone as L-mode, wherein "the goal is to enhance long-term competence. Activities have to involve 'not perfect yet' knowledge and skills—things you can improve on." This mode of thinking stands in stark contrast to defensive mode, in which your self-worth is under attack. It also counterbalances performance mode, in which the goal is a flawless performance at all costs. All three modes, or zones, have their place in the classroom. But the learning zone is where we want our students to be most of the time. Encourage conditions that enable learners to have great success, and great failure, in the safety (and fun) of the learning zone.

Conclusion

A project launch is a transfer-level experience that requires simple, doable teacher habits to ensure that the launch remains sustainable. Teaching to transfer can be a challenge, and these habits are meant to help teachers navigate that challenge. Overall, they will ensure clarity of the content-based learning intentions versus activities, contexts, and student work structures. Moreover, this phase is setting the tone for the type of culture that we want in our learning spaces and future work environments. Students will interact with each other, offer suggestions, and co-construct the purpose, expectations, and next steps for the journey ahead. Teachers balance advocacy of the learning expectations and inquiry of the questions and next steps along the way. This phase is critical to forming the rationale for the other phases and setting the tone and tenor for the future work of the class. River City awaits. See an example launch showcase at the end of this chapter.

Review Questions

❋ What successes and challenges do you see with engaging in the habits related to a rigorous launch?

☛ How are you currently starting students with a challenge? How are you using entry events and engaging in co-construction of expectations? To what extent are you using sequential or integrated launches? What may be the next steps in this habit?

☛ How are you working with students to "name the gaps" between what is expected and where they are currently in their learning?

☛ How do you currently support students in "looking ahead" in their learning?

✳ Which action habit(s) for a project launch seem(s) most doable for you right now? Why? What next steps can you take to leverage your strengths in this area?

✳ Which habit(s) seem(s) most doable for students right now? Why? What next steps can you take to leverage their strengths in this area?

✳ Which entry event activity (GRASPS, matrices, Four Act Tasks, or Gap Analysis) are you going to use to launch students into transfer-level expectations?

✳ Which habit(s) seem(s) most challenging for you right now? Why? What next steps can you take to build your capacity, lower your perceived concerns, or support yourself in attempting these habits?

🏃 Next Steps

Before starting a full-on project, implement a few of the habits in Phase 1. Give yourself and your students the opportunity to develop familiarity with how they work. Below are a few suggested next steps to consider:

✳ Launch a unit using an entry event.

✳ Select and implement one habit with your students. During the implementation, record your observations of student engagement.

☛ **Behavioral:** What did you notice about students when they were on task? What did they do well with following the protocol? Where did they struggle? What do you infer are the reasons students succeeded or struggled with specific parts of the protocol?

☛ **Emotional:** How did students interact with each other? Did students seem to care about the activity or the topic?

☛ **Cognitive:** Did students gain new knowledge, make connections, or apply their understanding to a new situation? What evidence are you using to answer this question?

❋ Use a co-construction strategy (see Table 3.6) outside of a project context and then reflect on the process with students. Reflection questions include:

☛ To what extent did we understand why we were co-constructing a driving question or success criteria?

☛ How long did the process take? How might that change with repeated practice?

☛ How did this impact our understanding of the success criteria or driving question?

❋ Use a K/NTK list with your students outside of a project context. This will develop everyone's familiarity with the process.

☛ Integrate with a pre-assessment.

☛ Designate the last five to ten minutes of the learning block to revisit the knows/need-to-knows on a regular basis.

☛ Try breaking up the K/NTK list into surface, deep, and transfer levels.

🚀 Launch Showcase

Applying a Hexagonal-Thinking Approach in Rigorous PBL

While the main text of this book offers a number of different approaches to launch a project, another creative way to kick-start a project with students is called the hexagonal-thinking approach (HTA).

The HTA process tasks students with engaging in all levels of learning (i.e., surface, deep, and transfer learning) at the beginning of the project. The HTA process consists of six steps that task students with generating potential driving questions by evaluating multiple contexts and distinguishing between content and contexts (transfer) as well as finding connections between ideas (deep learning) and identifying core concepts (surface learning). This process enables teachers and students to engage in habits that encompass Phase 1 of the PBL process, which include:

Habit 5 - Start with a challenge

Habit 6 - Name the gaps

Habit 7 - Look ahead

Since a hexagon has six sides, it's a useful symbol for remembering each of the six steps of the HTA. (See Table 3.11.)

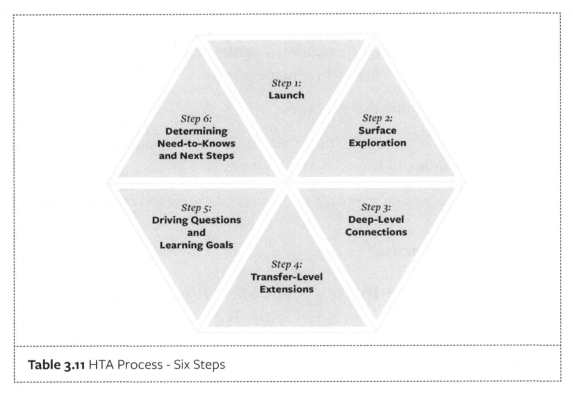

Table 3.11 HTA Process - Six Steps

Step 1: **Launch** - Provide a challenging context (or set of contexts) to initiate intellectual engagement for students. In PBL, we often call this an entry experience or an entry event.

The example below is related to the study of evolution and could be used across a range of grade levels:

Example:

> When students walk into the first class of a unit about endangered species, evolution, or ecosystems, they are tasked with watching a controversial video about de-extinction. They begin by watching "Hunted to Zero" (see QR code below), and continue by exploring the accompanying website: https://colossal.com/de-extinction/

Figure 3.3 Video - "Hunted to Zero"
Source: Colossal.com

Step 2: **Surface Exploration** - Provide students with a set of hexagonal shapes (e.g., set of hexagonal sticky notes) that enable them to write down key terms that are important from the initial launch. Share with students that one color should represent contexts (situations in which the content applies) and one color should represent the content (specific knowledge or skills that students must learn and apply to other situations). One scaffold that may be helpful to initiate this process is to provide students with a set of content-based and contextual terms to begin drafting hexagonal tiles.

Example:

> In the de-extinction example, students are provided with a mixture of contextual scenarios and content-based terms and are tasked with writing down each idea on hexagonal tiles. For instance, *Jurassic Park*, *Theranos*, and *cloning* would be examples of contexts and would be written in one color. *Amino acids*, *genes*, and *DNA* are all content-based outcomes written on another set of hexagons with a different color from the contextual hexagons. In this example, the teacher has offered terms in genetics and cell biology because those have been learned in previous units. The teacher

could have used terms such as *speciation, adaption,* and *Hardy-Weinberg* to identify student understanding of terms yet to be covered in class.

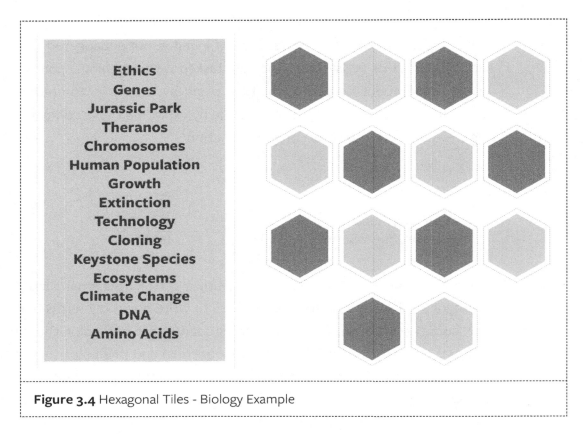

Figure 3.4 Hexagonal Tiles - Biology Example

Note: To access hexagonal tiles, the authors recommend the following solutions:

1. Order hexagonal sticky notes and have them laminated for continued use.

2. Use Pam Hook's Hexagonal Tile generator (Hook, n.d.) and have students work out the tiles online. This resource link is provided in the online Appendix.

Step 3: **Deep-Level Connections** - This step is conducted in two parts or substeps. During part 1, students are tasked with finding connections between hexagons they have labeled. Additionally, students write down a few sentences on the connections between content, between contexts, and across both content and contexts. Please note that when students are comparing content, they are engaging in deep learning, and when they are comparing contexts, they are engaging in transfer learning. As such, both processes are occurring during this step.

During part 2, with one another or in groups, students compare and contrast their hexagon structures and rationale for each connection.

Example:

> In the de-extinction project, students are tasked with putting their hexagons together where they see connections (see Figure 3.5). Next, they are asked to write down why they made those connections. See an example of what students may write down to explain their thinking (Table 3.12).

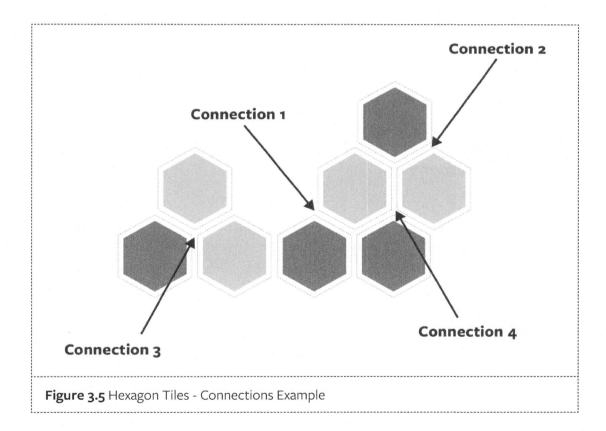

Figure 3.5 Hexagon Tiles - Connections Example

Explain your thinking

Connection # 1. Extinction and Human Population Growth - Extinction and human population growth have a positive correlation.

Connection # 2. Cloning and Technology - The use of technology has given humans the ability to create clones of different species and afforded opportunities (as well as pitfalls) to the frontier of cell destruction.

Connection # 3. Extinction and Keystone Species - We looked up keystone species, and it looks like if they die out, other species may die as well.

Connection # 4. DNA and Chromosomes - Chromosomes are the packages that hold DNA.

Table 3.12 Explain Your Thinking Hexagon Tiles - Student Example

Next, students will evaluate and reflect on the similarities and differences between their hexagonal configurations and those of other student groups (see Figure 3.6).

What similarities and differences emerge between group configurations?

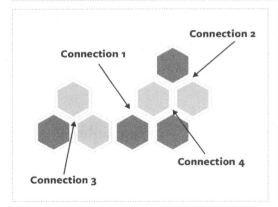 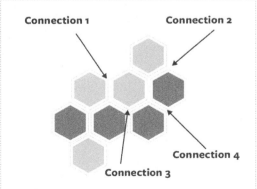

Figure 3.6 Hexagon Tiles - Similarities and Differences

Similarities across groups	Differences across groups
~ Both groups found connections between keystone species and extinction. ~ Both groups identified Jurassic Park and Theranos as contexts. ~ Both groups agreed that human population growth was related to extinction.	~ The other group connected climate change, ecosystems, and human population growth together in a cluster. We didn't have all these concepts connected. ~ We considered cloning content, and they considered it a context.

Table 3.13 Hexagon Group Connections - Similarities and Differences

Step 4: **Transfer-Level Extensions** - Ask students to generate additional contexts and/or content to consider in this project. This is an opportunity to prompt students to create analogies, compare contexts within and across groups, and generate hypotheses on how their configurations will change over time. This is also an opportune time for students to begin drafting questions they want to solve.

Example:

In the de-extinction example, students are tasked with adding additional contexts and potential content that could be added to the hexagonal configuration. To generate new contexts, teachers ask students to generate analogies. For example, *What other examples can you think of where humans have manipulated natural processes? Do any stories, movies, or situations come to mind?*

Next, students walk around the room and observe the various contexts that other groups have generated. Here the teachers prompt students to write down answers to the following questions: What contexts are unique around the room? What contexts are common? What patterns emerge? What questions come up for you?

Step 5: **Driving Questions and Learning Goals** - Using the power of conversation, students should work together to identify the overall driving question, learning intentions, and success criteria. One way to do this is to use structured protocols (e.g., chat stations).

Example:

In the de-extinction project launch, students are placed into four groups that will mix and match with others over the course of four discussions. In this example, the teacher uses a chat station (see Gonzalez, 2013) to structure the conversation with students. The link to the blog post is provided in the online Appendix for additional information regarding the chat station protocol. The questions for each station are listed below for students to address.

❋ Perspectives (Chat 1): What are potential perspectives that emerge from this problem? What is your current position on this problem? What else would you want to know about this situation?

❋ Problem (Chat 2): What do you see as potential driving questions from the connections made between different groups?

❋ Potential Outcomes (Chat 3): What do you think we will need to learn to address these questions and to understand the connections more deeply?

❋ Patterns and Potential Connections (Chat 4): What other contexts can you think of that connect to this work? Do you see any recurring patterns? (See Figure 3.7.)

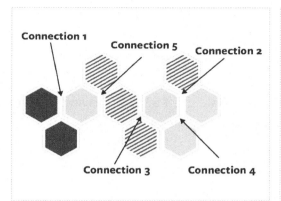
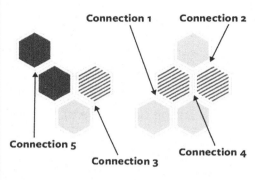

Perspectives (Chat 1): What are potential perspectives that emerge from this problem? What is your current position on this problem? What else would you want to know about this situation?

Problem (Chat 2): What do you see as potential driving questions from the connections made between different groups?

Potential Outcomes (Chat 3): What do you think we will need to learn to address these questions and to understand the connections more deeply?

Patterns and Potential Connections (Chat 4): What other contexts can you think of that connect to this work? Do you see any recurring patterns?

Figure 3.7 Hexagon Tiles - Chat Station

Step 6: **Determining Need-to-Knows and Next Steps**

During this final step, students and teachers determine which driving question or set of questions they will work to answer. As a part of answering this question, teachers provide the rubric and ask students to compare and contrast their thinking of what they are learning with that of the teacher. Next, students draft any next steps they will take to answer the driving question(s) and meet the learning intention(s) and success criteria. Finally, students generate hypotheses on how their hexagonal configurations will change over time.

Example:

In the de-extinction project, the students draft a set of driving questions using one of the of the following stems:

❉ To what extent…

❉ Should…

❉ Where…

❉ When…

Next, students evaluate the teacher's content-specific rubric with learning intentions and success criteria and write down what they labeled on the hexagonal tiles that was also on the rubric using a structured protocol (see Table 3.14—"Got it!").

Next, the students generate key questions or need-to-knows to meet expectations on the rubric. The teacher then returns to the driving questions and asks for any additional revisions. The students then choose one question to work on during this project.

Students then draft next steps for their learning. The teacher also asks students to take a picture of their hexagons as they will make a hexagon in the middle and at the end of the project and reflect on those changes.

Got it I already understand or can do…
Gaps I do not understand or am unable to complete…
Need-to-Knows I wonder…

Next Steps
1.
2.
3.
4.
5.

Table 3.14 Hexagon Tiles Student Reflection Template

To learn more about hexagonal thinking the authors suggest Pam Hook's 2022 book *SOLO Taxonomy and Hexagonal Thinking: Using Hexagons to Think Critically, Creatively, and Collaboratively.*

Chapter 4

PHASE 2: BUILDING KNOWLEDGE

> " Human beings are not built in silence, but in word, in work, and in action-reflection.
>
> —Paulo Freire

A single and paradoxical habit constitutes Phase 2: develop surface-level knowledge and skill. It is singular because, yes, it is that simple and it is certainly that important. The paradox lies in this: most educators who choose project-based learning do so because of its movement *away* from surface-level learning. We gravitate toward a PBL model because we crave the thrill of relevance, coherence, and high-level application. If the majority of traditional teaching and learning is carried out at the surface level, habitually challenging students to transfer their understanding to situations that matter is an attempt to buck the trend.

The truth is, teaching surface-level knowledge will never leave classrooms and it never should. Learners need the basics. It's where they will start, but it cannot be where they end. Without encompassing vocabulary words, places on a map, or simple procedures, students' understanding will be empty. Students will create beautiful presentations and innovative models but be unable to explain their thinking. Moreover, in the absence of surface learning, those who come to class with previous exposure to a topic will make connections based on what they already know. They will confirm our bias that we have made all the right instructional choices, while those students who come to class with less preexisting knowledge will leave our tutelage not much better than they started.

In the foreword of *Rigorous PBL by Design,* John Hattie shared a study illustrating the variance in student learning in medical school using PBL. The study clearly identified which students benefited from PBL and which did not. Fourth-year medical students, who had already developed expertise, thrived when they were given a problem to solve together. First-year students, however, flopped. They showed little to no growth in the PBL classroom relative to their peers who received direct instruction. The cautionary tale here is that PBL is a suitable method for experts but not a good fit for novices.

In keeping with this "good for experts but not for novices" mindset, some may argue that PBL is best left to students on an accelerated path. This is a slippery slope of perception that has implications for educational equity. It suggests that privileged students can be taught how to think but that those who are less advantaged should be held to a lower standard. We disagree. In *Rigorous PBL by Design* (2017), the argument was made that if we embed direct instruction and other surface-level instructional strategies, all students can gain access to rigor and relevance.

This chapter reviews the habit of building basic knowledge. Moreover, the chapter distinguishes direct instruction from didactic teacher-led talking and discusses how direct instruction can be effectively utilized in the RPBL process.

Phase 2: Surface-Learning Workshops

Rigorous PBL Teacher Habit	Success Criteria
Habit 8: **Build the foundation** by applying instructional and feedback strategies to support surface-level learning	~ Apply surface-level instruction to support student learning ~ Use appropriate feedback strategies to enhance student learning

Table 4.1 Teacher Habits and Success Criteria during the Building-Knowledge Phase

Habit 8: **Build the foundation** *by applying instructional and feedback strategies to support surface-level learning*

How do learners continue with the co-learning and rich discourse of the project launch and still address the basic knowledge and skills of a discipline? The three habits that make up Phase 1 of Rigorous PBL by Design include co-construction, honest discourse, and transfer-level expectations from the word go. They depend on dialogue about the distance—or nearness—of current understanding in relation to learning intentions. In a different context, this may appear to be a habit that teachers need to shake if we are to move beyond surface-level learning as our primary stance. But this phase of the project is nonnegotiable. An understanding of the basics is crucial for students to fully experience deep and transfer learning.

Surface learning can integrate just as much discourse, challenge, and discussion as the project launch. In fact, it probably should. Frequent opportunities to summarize, practice, and relate the learning to prior knowledge help make sure learners are *with* rather than simply being spoken *to* as they construct basic understanding.

Instructional strategies and feedback specifically enacted to bolster surface-level learning should also become a matter of habit for this phase in the project. Following the co-constructing and divergent thinking that characterizes Phase 1, Phase 2 is a time for dialogue between teachers and learners to be precise, straightforward, and direct. This convergent learning will ensure all learners are prepared to return to the divergent thinking patterns required as the project continues (see Figure 4.1).

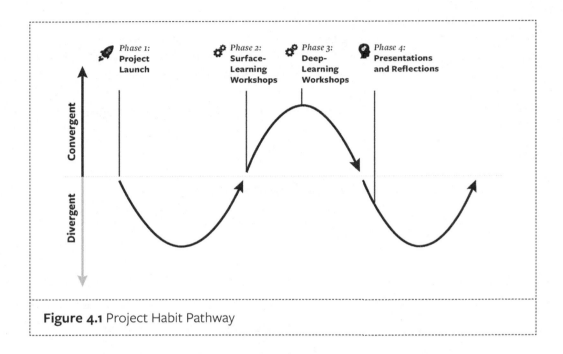

Figure 4.1 Project Habit Pathway

The workshop model can shape learning blocks or class periods into a rhythm that makes sense. It gives teachers and students time to learn, rehearse, and make meaning. Workshop models can vary in the details of what each section is called, how those sections are broken down, and the duration of each. Put simply, a workshop consists of three parts that many teachers will find familiar and practical: a short lesson, practice, and debrief (see Figure 4.2). This model can be utilized at various stages of learning, but for this chapter, the focus will be for surface-level understanding.

DNA of a Workshop

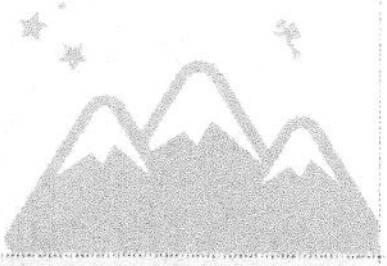

	Level of learning:		
	 Surface	 Deep	 Transfer
Review what students know and need to know			
Mini-Lesson (10 minutes) — **Make a connection**			
Provide instructional strategy			
Independent Work Time with Teacher Conferring (25–35 minutes) — **Provide opportunities for practice**			
Debrief (8–10 minutes) — **Review what students learned and what they need to know**			
Inspect outcomes from work time (through shares and discussion)			

Figure 4.2 Workshop Schema

Success Criteria: *Apply surface-level instruction to support student learning*

If surface-level teaching and learning tends to be the default mode in many classrooms, why should we name it as a habit to be developed? It's about doing the right thing at the right time. When direct instruction is used as students build knowledge, it's a powerful strategy. In addition, just because it works well for surface learning doesn't mean this phase and deep learning are mutually exclusive. For example, asking open-ended questions that build on concrete knowledge and skills can help usher students into deeper thinking while they are still building foundational skills. To borrow a metaphor from Mehta (2018), stages of learning are less like a ladder and more like a web. Even as students are building basic skills, their learning is embedded in the larger scheme of the project challenge.

Students must be active in this process. It is their minds, after all, that require rehearsal and deliberate practice in order to consolidate their understanding. There are many ways that students can acquire learning surface-level knowledge and skills. Identifying ways for students to preview information, participate in constructing knowledge, and represent their learning can be a helpful way for teachers to strategize regarding the surface-learning workshop. Table 4.2, adapted from Marzano's (2017) *The New Art and Science of Teaching*, shows strategies that can be embedded in this phase of learning:

Preview and Predict	Present and Participate	Representing and Reflecting Learning
~ Know/need-to-know list ~ Preview questions ~ Brief teacher summary ~ Teacher-prepared notes	~ Direct instruction ~ Reciprocal teaching ~ Jigsaw ~ Concept attainment ~ Elaborative interrogations	~ Notes ~ Graphic organizers ~ Dramatic enactments ~ Mnemonic devices ~ Employing imagery ~ Outlining ~ Summarizing ~ Giving and receiving corrective feedback

Table 4.2 Embedded Strategies in Direct Instruction
Source: Adapted from Marzano, 2017.

It may surprise some teachers to see direct instruction listed as a recommended choice. In fact, direct instruction is critical to effective rigorous PBL. Contrary to "guide on the side" teaching, which relies on creating conditions where students will discover what they need to learn, direct instruction presumes that all students are capable of developing proficiency when they are explicitly taught. Moreover, it's a solid practice for efficiently teaching learners foundational knowledge and skills. Direct instruction (Hattie, 2009, 2021) has a considerable effect size (ES .59) and is based on the following quality criteria:

* ❋ Clear learning intentions and success criteria are reviewed

* ❋ Success criteria are tied to long-term aims (in this case, the problem or project)

* ❋ Frequent modeling and checking for understanding

* ❋ Guided practice between the teacher and student

* ❋ Independent deliberate practice to reinforce understanding

One important consideration to note here is the importance of dialogue within direct instruction. It is all too easy, as the teacher, to tell and profess, then move on. "I told you last week, so you should know it now" goes the teacher's retort. In this case, we make assumptions based on what we think learners *should* understand rather than frequently checking what they *do* understand. Direct instruction at its best, however, leverages small bites of teacher talk with ongoing dialogue between peers and between teachers and students. Rather than the teacher as a soloist, the entire classroom is a symphony.

Before, during, and after surface-level lessons, it is critical that teachers remind students of the bigger picture of the learning journey. Students are not learning mnemonics, outlining, and practicing problems on a worksheet in isolation. Rather, these routines are connected to larger goals, questions, and tasks. Moreover, these connections should not be presented to students but rather actively discussed.

For teachers or administrators who are concerned about the amount of teacher talk that is implied by direct instruction, being keenly aware of talk in the classroom can prevent a didactic approach. Teachers can make sure the time for the input portion of a lesson is of equal to or less than that for modeling and checking for understanding. This ensures that students are doing their share of working with the material at hand. Consider the steps in Table 4.3: when designing for surface-learning workshops.

Step	Description	Level of Learning Strategy
Review clear learning intentions and success criteria	Clarify learning intentions and success criteria. *"Today we are continuing to learn about . . ."* *"You'll know you're successful if you can . . ."* Or *"Today we are continuing to learn . . ."* *"We're working on our surface-level success criteria, but there may be a few times today when we are going into the deep . . ."*	Anchor: Clarity (ES .75) Anchor: Success Criteria (ES .88)
Make a connection	Connect to the driving question or project: *"Let's review why we are going to learn about ratios. What's the big picture? Why is this a need-to-know for us?"*	Integrating Prior Knowledge (ES .93) Planning and Prediction (ES .76)

Step	Description	Level of Learning Strategy
Instructional strategy	~ Input (critical surface knowledge is provided through a variety of mediums—lecture, video, podcast) ~ Modeling (labeling, categorizing, and comparing examples and nonexamples) ~ Checking for understanding (monitoring and taking action on student evidence of "doing it right")	Surface: Direct Instruction (ES .59) Deep: Evaluation and Reflection (ES .75) Anchor: Giving and Receiving Feedback (ES .71)
Independent practice	Students practice and demonstrate proficiency. Teachers monitor and provide feedback and remediation; students may work with others on giving feedback.	Surface: ~ Deliberate Practice (ES .77) ~ Spaced versus Massed Practice (ES .60) ~ Outlining and Transforming ES .85) ~ Mnemonics (ES .76) ~ Rehearsal and Memorization (ES .73) ~ Help Seeking (ES .60) Deep: ~ Elaboration and Organization (ES .75) ~ Seeking Help from Peers (ES .83)

Step	Description	Level of Learning Strategy
Closure	Reinforce key points, eliminate confusion through clarification, and form a coherent picture of the learning. *"Before we leave today, let's review the key learning from today and how it connects to our project goals."*	Surface: Summarizing (ES .66) Deep: ~ Classroom Discussions (ES .82) ~ Evaluation and Reflection (ES .75) ~ Strategy Monitoring (ES .71)

Table 4.3 Direct Instruction Instructional Layout

Note for exceptional learners: When the teacher does most of the talking, students who have less access to learning strategies and positive self-talk are the ones who are the most negatively affected. Learners need opportunities to summarize their understanding or articulate their points of confusion; when these opportunities are in short supply, students who are disengaged or confused undergo little change. They remain "in the learning" without a way to recover. On the other hand, those students who have the cultural capital to play the game of school will persist despite a learning block spent in silence. Checks for understanding, reciprocal teaching, and summarizing support all learners—but especially those who have the greatest needs.

Success Criteria: *Use appropriate feedback strategies to enhance student learning*

If deliberate practice is the glue that makes surface learning stick, feedback is the activator that makes the glue stick better and in the right place. Take, for example, the story of a runner training after an injury. After a fracture, her trainer prescribes exercises that will build strength and flexibility in the injured leg. She faithfully repeats the exercises five times per week, and over time, she begins to see gradual improvement. However, she plateaus until a regular visit with her trainer, who watches her do the simple exercises and interjects to correct her form. As soon as she makes this slight correction, everything snaps into place: muscles that were at rest are suddenly taught, and balance that had seemed easy gives way to wobble at the immediate challenge. This is the real exercise that had been prescribed, and the one that will yield the healing she needs. Corrective feedback, given in the moment, is what can make the difference between mediocre repetition and exceptional results.

In the same way, feedback offered when students are building surface-level knowledge is essential. A core part of effective direct instruction is the use of effective feedback during the checking for understanding, guided practice, and review portion of the lesson.

For the surface stage of learning, key practices that are critical for providing effective feedback include:

❋ **Reduce the noise:** Relate feedback directly to the success criteria, not the learner (see Table 4.4).

❋ **Right on time:** Provide feedback during the lesson and independent practice.

❋ **With plenty of time:** Give learners time to apply the feedback they just received.

❋ **Quick and direct:** Corrective feedback is the most valuable during surface learning; at this stage, learners need to know if they got it right or if they've made an error.

Additionally, it is appropriate to validate students' work when they are adhering to the success criteria correctly. As students develop their early skills and understanding, it is just as valuable for them to hear that they are right as it is for them to hear that they need to make a change.

Examples of corrective feedback

The verb here should be *estar* instead of *ser*. When you describe Lilea's feeling, you're describing something that is temporary—so it's *Ella está feliz*. Later, she's furious, right? In that case, it's a temporary feeling again, so will you use *ser* or *estar*?

The lowercase *h* is a tall letter. The top needs to start all the way at the "sky" of your handwriting lines, and right now it looks a little short.

Our first success criteria is to distribute the number outside parentheses to the equation inside parentheses. Here I see your *3* was distributed to the X and you also multiplied it by the *7* that was in the equation. That's right.

Table 4.4 Corrective Feedback Examples

As mentioned earlier, the stages of learning are more like a web than a straight single line. Learners will often move between different stages of surface, deep, and transfer as they acquire a skill or knowledge. There is no one-and-done questioning stem or strategy for feedback during this second phase of the project. It is helpful to prioritize corrective feedback here, but teachers may find freedom in noticing different students' levels of understanding and differentiating their feedback accordingly.

We know that, especially with a variety of students in the room, learning isn't static. Our feedback doesn't need to be static either. A teacher's awareness of the ebb and flow of learning is key to offering the right kind of feedback at the right time. In the same way that instructional strategies will be specific to surface knowledge but may also integrate moments of relating this knowledge (deep) and applying it to a new context (transfer), feedback will often be corrective (surface) but may also be about learners' process (deep) or a question of self-regulation (transfer). Comfort with this fluidity takes time and practice. Examples of feedback prompts at three different levels are provided in Table 4.5.

Task	Process	Self-Regulation
~ Is the answer correct or incorrect? ~ Does the answer meet the success criteria? ~ What was done well here? ~ What went wrong here?	~ What is the explanation for the correct answer? ~ What strategies were used? ~ What other information is provided that could help? ~ How does this relate to other parts of our work?	~ What would you do differently next time? ~ How does this compare to . . . ? ~ How have your ideas changed? ~ What can you now teach? ~ What happened when . . . ?

Table 4.5 Task, Process, and Self-Regulation Feedback Question Examples

Additionally, feedback doesn't only transpire between students, or from the teacher to the student. Feedback from the students to the teacher during this phase can also be incredibly valuable. If we are truly to create a culture where student voice is amplified, soliciting learners' input can significantly shape a teacher's next instructional choices. During independent practice, teachers may circulate not only to answer questions but to ask questions of their own. What will you do first? or "What do you mean by . . . ?" will give feedback to the teacher about students' current understanding. These open-ended questions can yield valuable information about the impact of the lesson and where the class is succeeding or has misconceptions.

Research suggests that most questioning in the classroom requires answers that take less than three seconds to deliver, which will give limited feedback to the teachers. The typical questioning that asks, "Who can tell me the answer to . . . ?" will reveal only what is known by the student who is called on (Hattie & Timperley, 2007). Making it a part of regular practice to move about the room and seek genuine understanding of what students know ensures that the benefits of feedback go both ways. Teachers and students both try, act, and interject, until harmonious learning snaps into place.

🔆 Conclusion

When compared to the momentum built in Phase 1, learning basic knowledge doesn't need to feel like moving from fireworks to flash cards. High-quality direct instruction will include frequent checks for understanding, student discourse, and just-in-time feedback. The challenge with Phase 2 is to ensure that you don't stay here too long. Surface-level learning is an important part of the journey, but it isn't the final destination. Inquiry plays a role in this phase and it is perhaps best to lean on that role. As learners move back and forth between different levels of learning, teachers may also move into the third project phase and find times that they need to revisit the habit they leveraged in Phase 2. Here is where we make good on our expectations that all students receive excellent first instruction so they can reach farther and deeper as their learning continues.

❓ Review Questions

* After reviewing Table 4.2, what are the similarities and differences between your approach to direct instruction and what is discussed in this chapter? Where do you see potential opportunities for enhancing direct instruction to support student learning?

* What success criteria for this habit are you already executing?

* How could you layer new moves into your preexisting habits around surface-level knowledge (e.g., set plays, stacking; for more information on developing habits, please read Chapter 7)?

* How can you ensure a balance of both feedback to the student and feedback to the teacher?

Next Steps

❋ Layer an opportunity to ask your students open-ended feedback questions in an effort to analyze your own impact during surface-level lessons.

❋ Create a set play for monitoring teacher talk versus student action, and find a way to be held accountable for engaging in the right balance over time.

❋ Determine a strategy for going back and forth between task-related and process-related feedback.

Chapter 5

PHASE 3: DEEP-LEARNING WORKSHOPS

> " Struggling doesn't mean you are stupid; it means you are learning.
>
> —Guy Claxton

> " Belonging or being fully human means more than having access. Belonging entails being respected at the basic level that includes the right to both co-create and make demands on society.
>
> —john a. powell

Deep learning is associated with students developing an understanding of the relationship between single ideas (food chains) or skills (flutter kick) and unifying principles (thermodynamics) or practices (freestyle swim). Students also develop a greater level of proficiency in surface-level learning (single ideas or practices) and therefore are able to evaluate the strategies they are using to learn. These parallel skills of reflecting and evaluating our learning, while using critical thinking skills to understand unifying principles, are difficult to develop when learners are siloed. Research shows us that deep learning is largely developed in a social context. For instance, solicitation of help from peers and classroom discussions sit at the top of the most effective strategies in consolidating and unifying information and skills (Hattie & Donoghue, 2016).

Here you can listen in on students describing deep learning (see Figure 5.1). Notice how the students contrast deep learning and surface learning. Furthermore, observe the cues that are provided to support the students in navigating deep learning.

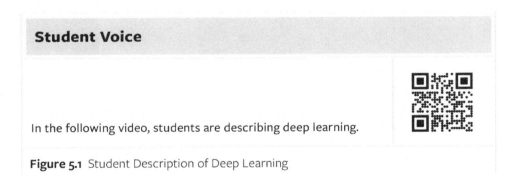

Student Voice

In the following video, students are describing deep learning.

Figure 5.1 Student Description of Deep Learning

In this phase, teachers are applying strategies that influence students deep learning. As discussed in Chapter 1, deep learning is substantially enhanced when students evaluate and reflect on relating core ideas of an academic discipline, engage in classroom discussions that promote critical thinking, and when students give and receive feedback from one another to improve their work and the work of others. Specifically, during deep learning students collectively engage in the following:

✳ Evaluate the similarities and differences between ideas or skills as a means to develop an understanding of themes or patterns in knowledge and skills

❋ Identify information that may be missing or is incorrect to better understand the general principles and practices of a learning outcome or set of outcomes

❋ Break down objects or ideas into simpler parts and find evidence to support generalizations

❋ Compile component ideas into a new whole or propose alternative solutions

❋ Make inferences drawn from a set of activities, including reading books, reviewing lab notes, observing patterns in a film scene, or conducting an interview

❋ Reflect on refining their own practices and that of their peers within the context of a learning culture

Impacting Deep Learning

The three most powerful strategies to enhance deep learning include classroom discussions, evaluation and reflection, and seeking help from peers (Hattie & Donoghue, 2016). Table 5.1 and Figure 5.2 illustrate specific teacher moves that enable students to engage in these strategies.

Classroom Discussions	Evaluation and Reflection	Solicitation of Help from Peers
~ Large-group protocols (e.g., Concentric Circles) ~ Small-group protocols (e.g., jigsaw) ~ 1:1 protocols (e.g., Think-Pair-Share)	~ Comparison strategies ~ Elaboration and organization ~ Examination of faulty logic ~ Identification of attacks, weak inferences, and misinformation ~ Integration with "breaking apart" (analysis) and "putting together" (synthesis) strategies	~ Strategy monitoring ~ Giving and receiving approximate feedback ~ Reflecting on performance and progress

Classroom Discussions	Evaluation and Reflection	Solicitation of Help from Peers

Table 5.1 Deep Teaching and Learning Strategies

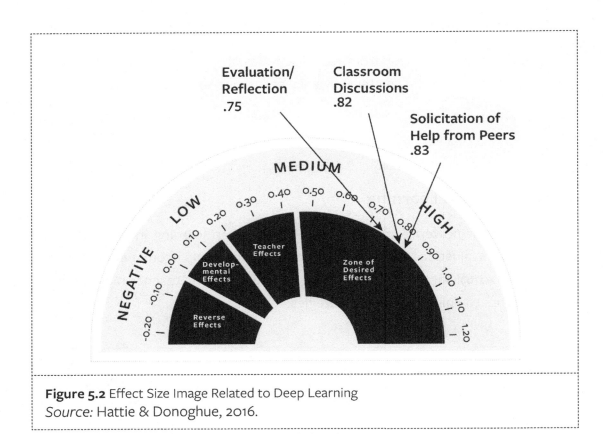

Figure 5.2 Effect Size Image Related to Deep Learning
Source: Hattie & Donoghue, 2016.

Deep-Learning Habits

Over the past two phases, students constructed clear expectations of learning and have developed a thorough understanding of the factual knowledge and procedural skills that serve as a building block for deeper learning. Phase 2 moved students to develop similar ideas about a subject area. This convergence is incredibly important to ensure everyone has a thorough understanding of a discipline. The crest of the convergence happens here where students develop an understanding of the underlying principles of the discipline. Interestingly, students also start to move to a divergent stage whereby they ask questions regarding the validity and reliability of what we know. They question ideas that may be laden with bias. Here, they tackle questions such as: Should we have dropped the atomic bomb? To what extent do we have a full understanding of the impact of manifest destiny? Why does there continue to be a debate on whether viruses are living? Why do we see only one point of view when we are learning about heroes? Who defines heroism? Why do we continue to find flaws in human logic? These questions are discipline specific and require students to weigh countering information. They challenge beliefs and perspectives that are often missing from classrooms where marginalized voices are missing.

In other words, deep-learning workshops enable students to solidify their understanding of core content and knowledge and begin to prepare for transfer-level learning.

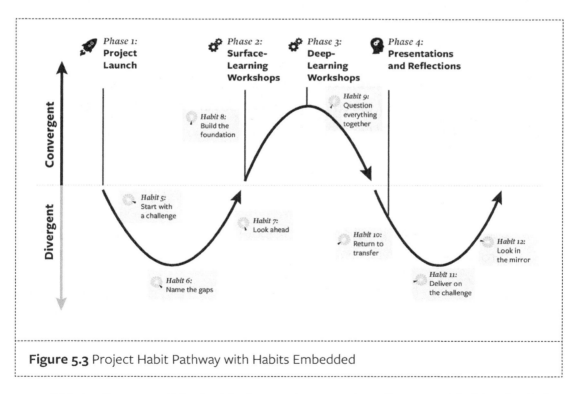

Figure 5.3 Project Habit Pathway with Habits Embedded

This is all accomplished with the routine practice of one core habit. This habit is shared in Table 5.2.

Rigorous PBL Teacher Habit	Success Criteria
Habit 9: **Question everything together** through structured discussions, deep-level feedback strategies, and formative assessments	~ Use collaborative protocols to promote shared power and deep learning through engaging in classroom discussions that evaluate and reflect on knowledge and skills ~ Use deep-level feedback strategies to enhance student learning by reflecting on progress, determining next steps, and improving peer-to-peer feedback ~ Incorporate assessments (formative, two-thirds, and final) into the learning process to promote reflection

Table 5.2 Teacher Habit 9 and Corresponding Success Criteria

Habit 9: **Question everything together** *through structured discussions, deep-level feedback strategies, and formative assessments*

Habit 9 is based on designing workshops that meet the deep-level strategies mentioned above. The habit includes the following success criteria:

✳ Use collaborative protocols to promote shared power and deep learning through engaging in classroom discussions that evaluate and reflect on knowledge and skills

✳ Use deep-level feedback strategies to enhance student learning by reflecting on progress, determining next steps, and improving peer-to-peer feedback

✳ Incorporate assessments (formative, two-thirds, and final) into the learning process to promote reflection

Success Criteria: *Use collaborative protocols to promote shared power and deep learning through engaging in classroom discussions that evaluate and reflect on knowledge and skills*

Collaborative protocols promote a concept of defined autonomy in a classroom. Defined autonomy may be defined as all students having voice and choice in their work *within the boundaries of common norms and agreements for belonging and dignity* and the content and skill expectations of the district. In one school, this idea is tied into the motto of the school: heart, mind, and action.

> **Heart:** We all have self-worth and carry with us humanity, which deserves respect. We all must create an inclusive environment in which everyone is respected.

> **Mind:** We are capable of learning and learning at high levels. This learning requires us to grow in our learning beyond surface-level knowledge to deep-to-transfer learning.

> **Action:** Rigorous and relational learning requires us to work together to meet the demands of the challenging work ahead of us.

We can stack heart, mind, and action by using collaborative protocols to engage in the critical thinking work involved in deep learning. A list of critical thinking skills can be found in the online Appendix.

Next, we want to align those critical thinking skills (e.g., evaluation, analysis, and synthesis) with a collaborative protocol. Stacking critical thinking skills with collaborative protocols to stimulate classroom discussions is highly recommended here. While not exhaustive, the protocols in Table 5.3 have been found to be easily adapted and used in K–12 classrooms around the world. You will notice that the collaborative protocols shown here have been presented in other chapters and are critical in Phase 4, presentations and reflections. The table below can also be found in the online Appendix, where it includes deep-learning tools to accompany protocols.

Purpose	Collaborative Protocols
Evaluation of content and skills	~ Carousel Brainstorm ~ Fishbowl ~ Concentric Circles
Analysis of content and skills	~ Chalk Talk ~ Four Corners ~ Socratic seminar
Synthesis of content and skills	~ World Café ~ Jigsaw ~ Classroom discussions

Table 5.3 Deep-Learning Skills and Protocols

Using any of the protocols above, or having students practice any of the critical thinking skills, can feel strange when they are still new. You may find, for example, that you overestimate the time that it takes for each pass of a World Café. That's okay. Classrooms are filled with wiggly bodies and imaginative minds; we all need permission to fail and try again. This is not business as usual—and that's why we're doing it.

To ease the classroom community into critical thinking and collaborative protocols together, the following process is recommended:

Before the protocol:

Review the purpose of the protocol and its process immediately before it is started. "Why are we doing this?" and "What will it look like?" are important questions to address at the outset so students can focus on the content of the learning. It's helpful here, if possible, for the teacher to model a mini-interaction with student volunteers. This can lower the anxiety of students who are worried they'll be put on the spot without understanding what they need to do.

During the protocol:

Conduct the protocol with fidelity. It's easy to slip into casual conversation or passively accept the first answer that is presented, but protocols exist to push groups beyond the first and easiest contributions. If the protocol is violated, stop the process so the class can discuss next steps to ensure the process is followed.

After the protocol:

Discuss the quality of the contributions and the distribution of contributions. "What did we do well today?" "What do we understand better now?" "How could we improve next time?" This deliberate pause sparks reflection about the group's process. Students should also independently reflect on the key content learning from the protocol. At the teacher's discretion, they may then share out with the entire class. The teacher should summarize key patterns from student discussions and add information to the need-to-know list.

Before moving to the next criteria, consider a few additional suggestions:

Just starting out:

If you are engaging in this habit for the first time, engage in a structured protocol with a small set of students and have everyone else observe. After the observation, have the entire class debrief the process. The suggested protocol for starting with a small group is the Fishbowl protocol and may be found in the online Appendix.

Well versed:

If incorporating deep-learning tools and collaborative protocols is a habit you have already established in your classroom, then students may be ready to conduct protocols in small groups interdependently (with teacher providing support). To do this, establish a small group of students as "process coaches." They will learn the protocol and conduct it with small groups. Your feedback will be directed to them regarding their conduct of the protocol. Over time, these roles are rotated and all students are able to independently conduct collaborative protocols.

Success Criteria: *Use deep-level feedback strategies to enhance student learning*

In the previous phase, most feedback was prescriptive—providing direct guidance to correct errors. As students develop content knowledge, the feedback that is required is less centered on the teacher and is focused on the quality of the discussion between the student requiring the feedback and the student(s) or teacher offering guidance.

The following videos feature students in primary and secondary schools who are prepared for feedback.

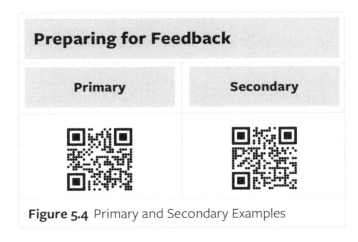

Figure 5.4 Primary and Secondary Examples

Beyond protocols, specific feedback strategies can promote deeper learning. Those strategies are outlined below.

Strategy 1: Nudge. As students gain proficiency, they are more able to use their existing knowledge to identify errors. At this point, they need less direct feedback related to their performance on a task and more feedback tied to their own ability to detect errors, monitor their performance, and find ways to take initiative. Provide just enough feedback for students to self-monitor and take action in their learning.

The following daily teacher actions help nudge students toward those dispositions.

✳ **One of many is incorrect:** In lieu of sharing with students which question is wrong and what to do, share that one of the responses is wrong or could be improved. Give the student a few minutes to inspect their own work and determine next steps. Have students share with you (or others) which answer was incorrect, why the error occurred, and next steps they will take to improve.

✳ **Sticky Notes protocol:** Provide corrective feedback on a few sticky notes for a group of students. Give the group those sticky notes and ask them to match each comment to its corresponding task. Listen to their level of clarity and feedback to each other.

✳ **Dots, not comments:** Place a dot near an error on a task and give the work back to the student. Once the student receives the work, share that the dots provide a clue for the place they need to improve. Debrief with the student after five or ten minutes to determine if they detected the error and how they fixed the problem. Focus your feedback on their efficacy of detection skills with their own work. (Did they analyze the task? Did they review work samples?)

Strategy 2: Establish social norms. Instead of shifting from teacher-centric feedback ("I do") to student-centric feedback ("you do"), establishing social norms is a way to focus on the learning-centered environment ("we do"). Ensure that collaborative agreements and processes are in place so that peer-to-peer feedback is accurate and helpful in students deciding next steps. With feedback, we need to shift away from the gradual release of responsibility to center on the need to cultivate a mutual responsibility of learning.

One way to start this work is by refining peer-to-peer feedback. Graham Nuthall's (2007) research has shown that students often receive and use feedback from their friends. Interestingly, he found that most peer feedback is inaccurate. We see this frequently played out in classrooms, in both formal and casual exchanges between students. How often do writing teachers see, for example, peer feedback focus on spelling errors rather than the deeper (and more challenging) concept of using relevant reasons to support a claim? Likewise, a common answer to "What do you do when you get stuck?" in higher-level math classes is often a shrug, followed by "I dunno. I text my friend." Peer-to-peer feedback happens constantly, with little guarantee that the feedback will be correct. To rectify this, we need to prepare students to give and receive accurate feedback.

We can support students by engaging in the following actions:

✳ **Group feedback protocols:** Establish a structured way for students to share their work and solicit helpful, specific feedback from a group of their peers. Examples include the Tuning protocol, Critical Friends, and TAG protocol in small groups (see the online Appendix). In these feedback conversations, students follow a simple structure in order to give and receive feedback. The teacher's role is to monitor the quality and accuracy of feedback.

✳ **Consultancy protocol:** Each student shares the challenge they are currently facing with a small group of students. Small groups review the student's current work and offer ways to help the student improve their learning. Establishing the norm of naming challenges, rather than hiding them, and inviting others to use inquiry to enhance the students' learning is a strong way to improve the whole group's achievement.

✳ **Game film:** Record students engaging in a presentation or discussion and have them watch themselves and others to reflect on their strengths, weaknesses, and opportunities.

As with collaborative protocols, consider whether teachers and students are just starting out or well versed in establishing social norms. For those just starting out, repeating one protocol for an extended period of time can help students build confidence. Classrooms that are more well versed can benefit from protocols that are led by students as "process coaches".

Strategy 3: Highlight nuance. Focus on range and/or subtle shifts in feedback to promote self-direction and prime creativity.

❋ **Divergent feedback:** Instead of corrective feedback, provide a set of questions that promote creativity. Ask: What would you do differently? How would your response change if the context or conditions changed?

❋ **Contextually different work samples:** Give students examples of exemplary work in different contexts or task types. For example, if students are focused on persuading others via a podcast, give them the opportunity to evaluate other forms of persuasion, including essays, debates, TED Talks, and the like.

❋ **Open success criteria:** If students have met the success criteria on a rubric, give them options to go deeper within the criteria. For example, consider students who may have met the success criteria of "Write a conclusion paragraph" in their essay. Go to those students who have met their objective and open the success criteria up for them by giving them the option to use a cliff-hanger or metaphor to conclude their work.

Strategy 4: Reflect on the impact of feedback on student learning with students. One of the most consistent things we see in the research about feedback is the importance of *how* it is received. Often, students don't realize that they were given feedback in the first place or don't understand that there is an expectation that they do something with it. Think of all the essays marked up with red ink that get only a brief glance and are tossed into the recycle bin. Moreover, the impact of feedback is greater when students feel that it is relevant to their progress. Providing the opportunity to respond to feedback, as well as reflect on how work improved as a result, is key to ensuring all the efforts put into feedback are worthwhile.

As students continue to take risks in the classroom, it is paramount that they stop and analyze their work. In doing so, learners invest in growing their capacity to identify their strengths and challenges, and create a plan for next steps. Again, protocols are extremely helpful during this process. One of the most powerful (and low-prep) strategies students can use to reflect on their own learning includes the What? So What? Now What? protocol. To do this, students might look at two versions of their work before and after feedback. This process could be accomplished independently, in small groups, or as a whole class. Students make straightforward observations to answer the question "What?" This is followed by inferences or explanations for why the work changed (or didn't) to discuss "So what?" Finally, "Now what?" is an invitation to formulate next steps based on what they see. See Table 5.4 for examples.

What? So What? Now What? – Lab Report
What: The conclusion was brief in draft #1, but we used academic vocabulary words like "velocity" and "increase" in the revised draft.
So what: The second draft conclusion is longer, makes more sense, and looks more academic. Feedback from my partner helped this improve. Also, my partner reminded me that one success criteria was to use academic vocabulary words in the conclusion.
Now what: Continue to include the academic vocabulary in lab reports and make changes when my partner gives me feedback—it makes my writing stronger!
What? So What? Now What? – Formative Quiz Scores
What: More than half of us couldn't solve the single-step equations in #s 6–10 on our first try. All but two of us were able to solve them the second time around.
So what: Taking notes during our lesson and checking to see if the first two questions were right, before we continued with our practice problems, helped us to know we were on the right track.
Now what: We know that just because we don't know something at first doesn't mean we can't learn it. We tried, asked for help, and learned well. Most of us are ready to put this together into a two-step equation. The two members of our class who are still having a hard time with this could line their notes up to their own work to see where they are stuck, ask peers for help, or work with the teacher during the intervention period.
Table 5.5 Using Protocols to Give and Receive Feedback

Success Criteria: *Incorporate assessments (formative, two-thirds, and final) into the learning process to promote reflection*

In this final success criteria for the habit of creating deep-learning experiences, timing is everything. During Phase 1, students took a pre-assessment and used that experience as a springboard to articulate their knows and need-to-knows. At this phase in the project, teachers and students have a prime opportunity to reengage in that discussion. Give students the chance to assess once more and show what they know when there is still plenty of calendar time left before a final assessment of learning. This is critical to making the protocols for deep learning worthwhile, as it will show students—and their teacher—how they've grown.

Creating the right environment to grow assessment-capable learners requires that students have dedicated times in class to identify where they are going, where they are now, and what's next. Brief formative assessments, such as exit tickets and entrance tickets, are efficient ways to embed quick checks that are intended *for the students*. But an intentional pause about two-thirds through the project calendar to assess all the knowledge or skills for the unit is a valuable reality check for the entire classroom community. Here's why the timing is important: the assessment isn't final. There is still time to reteach, embed more deliberate practice, or address misconceptions that may be widespread among students.

When an assessment two-thirds through mirrors the final assessment closely, learners get practice in showing what they know in a situation that is low stakes, meant to support rather than to dole out a final grade. The results may be encouraging, they may be full of happy surprises, or they may be a tough reality check. In any case, an honest look at where students currently stand can help move learners and teachers from "where we thought we were" to "where we actually are." Stick to an expectation of nonjudgment so that successes and failures can be seen for what they are: milestones on a road to learning.

Whether assessments fall into the category of brief formative or a two-thirds-through version of the final assessment, taking a thoughtful approach to reflection is helpful. Focus students on developing their self-efficacy, planning next steps to enhance growth, and supporting others in their learning. Table 5.5 shows some considerations.

Reflection...	Looks like:
On current progress relative to overall goals	**What am I learning?** **¿Qué estoy aprendiendo?** I can... use academic vocabulary words when speaking and writing. Yo puedo... utilizar palabras de vocabulario académico al hablar y escribir. Restate the words correctly / Repita las palabras correctamente — Use the words in sentences about what we're learning / Usa las palabras para completar oraciones sobre lo que aprendemos — Create new sentences that apply to something new / Crea nuevas oraciones que se apliquen a algo nuevo
On strategies	"That song we learned was goofy. But how many of us found ourselves resinging it in our heads, to make sure we were skip-counting accurately? What does that tell us about how we learn best?" "Is rereading notes sufficient to prepare us for activity or assessment? Or does it work better when we cover up the notes and quiz ourselves?"
Use of strategies to develop critical thinking skills	"Rather than just giving our partner the answer to the math problem, we practiced asking them a question instead. Did it work?"
Self-reflection · **I Used to Think/Now I Think (see example)** · **Gap Analysis** · **Student goal summary**	I used to think... Now I think...

Reflection...	Looks like:

Reflection with others
 	
· **Constructivist listening** (see example)
 	
· **Tuning**
 	
· **Learning Dilemma**
	Constructivist Listening
	
	Norms:
	I will:
	   • Listen and think about what you say
	   • Keep what you say confidential
	I will not:
	   • *Criticize you*
	   • *Give advice*
	   • *Break in with a personal story*
	
	Today's question:
	What are you confused or challenged by?

Table 5.5 Self- and Peer Assessment Examples

Note for exceptional learners: This can be a vulnerable experience when the gap between those who get it and those who don't widens. Some students may consistently need more time and practice. Something to keep in mind here is that nonjudgment can help create a safe space to openly and honestly discuss progress. Help students celebrate what they can do in relation to the success criteria, knowing—and holding expectations—that they, too, will see growth. Examine proficiency and growth in relation to the success criteria (not in relation to other students) in order to keep the conversation about clarity, and their ability to succeed, going strong.

Barriers to Deep Learning

If we as educators know this is where we want to go, why aren't we there yet?

At first blush, deep learning seems easy to implement. It looks easy from a design (or "motion") perspective, but research continues to show that in action we often (1) overscaffold the process, (2) struggle with sharing power as educators, and (3) are challenged by handling any and all vulnerability in the classroom. When these three forces combine, we often retreat to surface learning, where we can feel like we are in control, or we turn over power to students and have them work unguided toward transfer learning. Deep learning is the fulcrum of this work, yet things get in the way of creating a balance of power and learning. Let's review what stands in the way.

Overscaffolding to Avoid Desirable Difficulties

We often start executing deep-learning habits the right way and then slip into older surface-learning habits, breaking the activity down to make it easier for students. Akin to dieting, we do well in the mornings, but by the time we get to the end of our day, we relinquish and have the extra serving of chips and queso.

A number of studies have demonstrated that American teachers break down rigorous tasks and use habits of surface learning to relieve students who are struggling. In one study, teachers had developed procedural math problems (surface-level tasks) and problems designed to make connections (deep-level tasks). Despite their best intentions, teachers continued to break down the deep task into surface-level tasks. Here is a quote from a summary of that study:

> Rather than letting students grapple with some confusion, teachers often responded to their solicitations with hint-giving that morphed a making-connections problem into a using-procedures one. That is exactly what the charismatic teacher in the American classroom was doing. – (Epstein, 2019, p. 82).

We overscaffold for a variety of reasons, including:

Tension Point 1: Deep and transfer learning are *slow* and do not usually happen at the same time as initial teaching occurs. This is challenging because we desire instantaneous learning.

Deep and transfer learning are counterintuitive in that the learning often happens at a different time than the initial instruction. Delays in learning are a necessary ingredient for deep and transfer learning. This type of learning is the opposite of "before your eyes" progress; it is the anti—light bulb moment. The anti—light bulb moments are where meaningful innovative changes throughout history have occurred (Johnson, 2011).

The mantra here is that progress should not happen too quickly. If it does, we get what is called a knowledge mirage, whereby students can recite what they just learned but that information soon evaporates when it matters most. As such, long-run learning is most effective when learning is inefficient in the short term.

Tension Point 2: Transfer learning requires *confusion*, and we don't like difficulties that we can avoid.

While learning complex material requires time, it also requires students to be active in understanding core content. For example, copying notes in a math class creates very little difficulty for students because they simply need to mimic what the teacher is writing on the board. The notes provide a helpful reference when students engage in independent practice. But asking students to articulate each step of the problem using words instead of numbers (i.e., "distribute the -4"), connect each step to the success criteria, or even predict the next step in an unfinished problem requires conceptual understanding. Students must be active in these scenarios and may not know the correct answer right away. One way to do this is to have teachers consider how they can add obstacles to their teacher repertoire to make learning slower and more challenging and frustrating in the short term but better in the long run. Crucial to the success of these desirable difficulties is fostering a classroom culture where curiosity and mistakes are celebrated. Students' sense of belonging should remain strong even when the rightness of their answers is in question.

Tension Point 3: We praise teachers for our lack of confusion and ease of completing tasks, yet learning that lasts requires confusion and struggle.

Often we hear that problem- and project-based learning will be immediately embraced by students. The method is built on an idea of student engagement through real-world questions or scenarios, student ownership over making key decisions, and clear connections between what they are learning and their own lives. However, research has continually shown that students rank teachers who make work easier and clearer much higher than they do teachers who use more inquiry-based strategies. Epstein (2019) writes,

It is difficult to accept that the best learning road is slow and that doing poorly now is essential for better performance later. It is so deeply counterintuitive that it fools the learners themselves both about their own progress and their teachers' skills. (p. 90)

If an instructor tries a few different approaches to teaching some concept or material, she would likely conclude that the approach that leads to the most immediate and observable signs of student improvement is the best one. In fact, when teachers try to facilitate learning by making it as easy as possible, this may increase the immediately observable short-term performance, but it decreases the more important long-term retention. The fact is, our brains trigger more neural activity when confronted with an error than they do in the absence of cognitive dissonance (Moser et al., 2011). When things are not easy, our minds are primed for learning. In short, it is to our own detriment that we often seek to eliminate difficulties in learning. When learning is difficult, people make more errors, and they infer from this that the teaching method is ineffective.

The end of this chapter offers a few specific strategies that support teachers and students in engaging in desirable difficulties.

Avoiding Challenging Assumptions

Another reason for our natural inclination to pivot from deep learning and shift back to surface learning is that deep learning often requires students and teachers to wrestle with ideas that challenge their current reality. Students explore ideas that for them have been certainties growing up (e.g., American exceptionalism) and find that the ideas are flawed and the reality is much messier than originally thought. These concepts bring forward a number of different perspectives and nuanced understanding of information. Students must have tools to thoughtfully listen, advocate, and structure their thinking. Moreover, they need to be able to step back and evaluate and reflect on their own learning. How have they changed their original thoughts and ideas? What strategies seem to be effective in supporting their learning? How are they supporting and receiving support from peers?

Practicing Defined Autonomy

Teachers often find they are in a predicament when they have to find a way to share control in the classroom and allow a greater level of challenging perspectives (voice) and calls for action (choice). These dynamics push everyone to self-protect because the outcomes can be unpredictable. As teachers, we do our level best to ease students' frustration, but this type of frustration is the fuel to drive deep learning.

Overall, there are always good reasons to retreat from our plans to do great things. Deep learning is an important space for students to engage in and is the antidote to the pedagogy of poverty. Our work is to engage in great things with students by applying small shifts in our practice. When we do that, we meet excellence and equity. The opportunity gap can be mitigated here at deep learning.

The learning loss that has impacted so many students can be addressed here. This is the phase of interdependency. At its crux, we move from a convergence of knowledge and skills and diverge in how we use that knowledge and skill set across contexts. When students struggle to solve a problem or handle autonomy, we tend to ease the challenge for them. When these thoughts emerge for you, it is time to lean in and address the opportunity gaps that exist in our schools for deep and transfer learning. This chapter explored a key habit that when followed moves us toward a pedagogy of empowerment, engagement, and equity.

Practitioner's Note: *Incorporate habits to effectively support students in transitioning toward deep and transfer learning.*

The sets of strategies identified in Tables 5.6, 5.7, and 5.8 support students in deep and transfer learning, which include:

1. Strategies for slowing learning down

2. Strategies for infusing confusion

3. Strategies for bringing students (and parents) on board with deep and transfer learning

Strategy	Description	Application
Wait for an Answer	Allowing time to think between asking a question and requiring an answer gives students the opportunity to better formulate their answers and therefore increases the depth of answers. It also lets students know the instructor will not be answering his or her own questions. Even when generating incorrect answers, deep learning is promoted.	Use a protocol for students to process their thoughts with one another. Protocols such as Think-Pair-Share and discussion mapping are helpful for enabling students to generate answers.
Spaced Practice	Researchers have found that when teachers spiraled what they taught across the school year, students were more likely to retain material.	Integrate previously learned knowledge into introductory questions at the beginning/middle/end of a class period.

Strategy	Description	Application
Mind the Gap	Tolerate big mistakes and then weigh them with correct information.	Use protocols that require students to reflect on their progress over time, including I Used to Think/Now I Think and Gap Analysis.
Interleaving	Teach several skills or concepts in the same class rather than focusing on only one specific idea.	Ensure you are teaching across a range of complexity (Blooms, DOK) and/or connect to prior or future concepts that relate to what you are teaching.
Quiz Students	Quiz students on material rather than having them simply restudy or reread it. These can be low-stakes assessments, not necessarily related to a grade.	Provide low-stakes quizzes and have students analyze them with each other and share their learning with the class. Provide workshops on testing strategies students may use rather than passive rereading.

Table 5.7 Strategies to Slow Down Learning

Strategy	Description	Application
Active Creation of Material	Ask learners to generate target material through an active, creative process, rather than simply by reading passively. This could involve role playing—structured debates, puzzles, or scientific study (McDaniel & Butler, 2011).	Use co-construction strategies to support students in generating the key outcomes of the unit or lesson they are learning. A few strategies for co-construction may be found in online Appendix.
Change the Setting	Vary the settings in which learning takes place (Smith et al., 1978).	Increase the use of field trips, take short walk-and-talks around the school, visit new classrooms, go to the library, or explore the athletic spaces in the school.
Experience Confusion	When a concept is difficult, allow students to experience and work their way through their frustration. When students are able to resolve their initial confusion themselves, deeper learning takes place. This leverages the principle of making learning material less clearly organized (McNamara & Kintsch, 1996).	Provide curveballs—present students with changes to the situation they are studying. This may include changing the type of task, the context they are studying, or the perspective they are analyzing. In addition, offer structured protocols for students to process their frustration. Two protocols that come to mind here include the Charette protocol and Learning Dilemma.

Strategy	Description	Application
Challenge the Reader	When learners perceive that material is more difficult to read, they tend to read it with more care and process it more deeply (McNamara & Kintsch, 1996). Studies suggest that even using fonts that are slightly more difficult to read affects engagement and processing (Alter et al., 2007; Diemand-Yauman et al., 2011; Yue et al., 2013).	Provide students with work samples that show a variety of fonts, handwritten and typed.

Table 5.8 Strategies for Providing Confusion

Strategy	Description	Application
Clear Communications with Parents and Students Up Front	Parents and students should be a part of the conversation regarding desirable difficulties. The idea here is no surprises for what type of work students will be encountering in class. To do this, consider means of communicating out to stakeholders, the importance of desirable difficulties, and how they will show up in class.	Send communications home to parents that state that there will be times when their children will be confused and frustrated from the day. Share that these moments are important for their children to learn complex content and the tasks they are working on will not be linked with high-stakes grading. et them know that the mantra is "High challenge but low stakes."

Strategy	Description	Application
Ensure Work at Home Is of the Kind Variety	The recommendation here is to keep the desirable difficulties experienced within the boundaries of the school, where students have support. Work that goes home should be reinforcing skills students already know and can do.	Keep wicked work at school by providing homework to students that they already know how to do and that has instructions parents can easily follow.
Preparing for Challenge	Giving students a structured way to prepare for challenging work is helpful in building future habits to handle the emotions they will face in such a setting. The recommendation here is to give students structured protocols to prepare for challenging experiences.	Meet with students prior to a challenging experience and walk through a few exercises to handle potential frustration.
Stopping and Processing Challenge	Providing students with a midpoint break to step back and reflect on their progress or lack thereof can help students manage setbacks.	During the middle of challenging work, stop students and have them pair-share how they are feeling and what they can do to handle the current challenge.

Strategy	Description	Application
Reflecting on Difficulties	After students have completed a particular challenging experience, they need time to step back and reflect on their growth and setbacks.	Provide students an opportunity to share their experiences. Here we want to hear how students persevered, changed course, and managed their emotions.
Linking Learning over Time/Reflecting on Engaging with Difficulties over Time	Giving students the opportunity to reflect on multiple experiences throughout the year is beneficial for students to see the strategies they have used to navigate desirable difficulties.	Having students use a journal to collect their learning in wicked environments and then reflecting quarterly enables students to see their progress over time.

Table 5.9 Strategies for Bringing Students (and Parents) on Board with Desirable Difficulties

 Conclusion

In many ways, this is the most important phase. This phase anchors the whole notion of shared responsibility of learning and centers on the idea of "we do." Phase 3 should not be rushed; an investment in Habit 9 is central to long-term retention, high levels of engagement, and a mutual learning culture. As you leave this phase for the final phase of rigorous PBL, your opportunity to apply the habits enacted during Phase 3 to the next phase will increase the power of this model on student learning.

❓ Review Questions

* ❋ How do you currently support students in "questioning everything together"? What are nuanced approaches in this chapter that may be beneficial for you and your students?

⁎ To what extent are collaborative protocols used to promote classroom discussions that evaluate and reflect on knowledge and skills?

⁎ When do you use deep-level feedback strategies to promote student learning? To what extent are you differentiating feedback on a routine basis to meet student needs at deep and transfer levels of learning?

⁎ How do you incorporate assessments into the learning process?

⁎ Where do you see an area of growth? How could you layer new habits into your preexisting habits (e.g., set plays, stacking; see Chapter 7 for additional information on developing and sticking with habits)?

⁎ Where can you begin layering desirable difficulties into your classroom?

⁎ How can you increase student dialogue in your class and increase the quality of conversations to focus more on deep learning?

Next Steps

⁎ Select one of the key approaches to building up Habit 9.

⁎ Review Chapter 7 and create a plan for implementation.

⁎ Create a set play for the habit and find a way to be held accountable for engaging in the habit over time.

⁎ Determine a strategy for going back and forth between Phase 2 and Phase 3.

Chapter 6

PHASE 4: PRESENTATIONS AND REFLECTIONS

> " Knowledge is foundational. We agree. The problem with this argument is not that it's wrong; it is that it is only half-right.
>
> —James Mannion and Kate McAllister

The metaphor that the brain is like a computer or a muscle is simply wrong. The brain does not simply retain and regurgitate information, nor does it simply strengthen with grit and determination. The brain is like a magpie. Here is Paul (2021) describing the magpie as analogous to how the brain actually functions:

> Magpies—members of the corvid family, which also includes crows, jays, and ravens—are well known for making their nests out of whatever is available in the environment. The birds have been observed using an astonishing array of materials: not only twigs, string, and moss, but also dental floss, fishing line, and plastic Easter grass; chopsticks, spoons, and drinking straws; shoelaces, eyeglass frames, and croquet wickets. During the American Dust Bowl of the 1930s, which eliminated vegetation from huge swaths of the West, magpies' corvid cousins made nests out of barbed wire . . . Our brains, it might be said, are like magpies, fashioning their finished products from the materials around them, weaving the bits and pieces they find into their trains of thought...(p. 10)

We are collectors, scavengers, and builders of information through a wide array of our own thoughts, feelings, and experiences; those of others; and the environments in which we exist. We build together, and the materials we build with come from our intuition, our collective thoughts, and evidence of learning. We collect from authentic audiences, different contexts, peers, resources, and competing perspectives. As such, it is a false premise to treat the brain as a simple input-and-output machine. Truly learning about our impact as teachers and learners cannot be done in isolation from our ongoing lived experiences. Nor will it come through the sheer effort of following a rigid process to inspect our growth. This also means that no one person comes into the space as a computer or a super brain. Everyone—teachers and learners alike—comes in as a magpie and builds with what is in our space.

Did you know that a group of magpies is called a mischief? It is an apt name for the type of creative yet disciplined work students need to engage in transfer-level work. The past two phases enabled students to collect and consolidate knowledge and skills. This phase is a shift from depth of knowledge to breadth of contexts in which that knowledge is applied. Transfer learning is perfect for our magpie brains. This is where we build our nests from the conventional materials we find in curricula and also the unconventional materials surfaced by current events, student interests, and creative thinking.

This is the phase of the process where assembly and reassembly, and giving students new materials to think with, takes shape. Before we jump into Phase 4 and the action habits that ensure success, let's listen in on students discussing transfer.

Transfer Snapshot

Here we are again with the seventh-grade students we observed in Chapter 5. Here they walk through the language of transfer learning. After watching the video, go back to Chapter 5 and listen to the same students discuss deep learning. What differences do you notice between their descriptions of deep learning and transfer learning?

Student Voice

In the following video, students are describing transfer learning. Notice the cues that are provided to support the students in navigating transfer learning. What do you notice are the similarities and differences between deep and transfer learning?

Table 6.1 Transfer Learning Example and Question Prompts

In the earlier video, the students were studying homeostasis and how the various body parts they learned about at the surface level relate (deep learning). They developed an understanding of the body's remarkable ability to maintain balance, or homeostasis. At this point, the students are discussing the implications when the body's mechanisms to maintain homeostasis are tested. The test case for these students is outer space. They are applying their understanding of homeostasis to a specific context (transfer learning).

Imagine if these students were evaluating multiple contexts, including how the body responds deep under water, or to a novel viral infection, menopause, or specific types of cancer. Or go further and imagine if students reviewed how systems balance in an external context, such as the working of thermostats, various geological cycles, or supply-and-demand situations. Scanning these various contexts to pick up patterns, subtle differences, and potentially viable solutions for one or more problems is the work of transfer learning.

In other words, transfer learning is centered on breadth—being able to see across situations, problems, and solutions. Like the magpie, students learn to "think well" by having access to an array of situations that they can piece together to build their understanding. This level of thinking requires fundamentally different tools and strategies to support students in learning, practicing, and performing those skills in and out of the classroom.

Phase 4 Process and Overview

Phase 4 begins with reviewing the driving question(s) and scenarios along with a set of workshops that support the transfer level of learning. During this time, students are often working in small groups to work toward solutions to the driving question and the application of those solutions in one or more contexts. Small groups spend time engaging with authentic audiences and crafting presentations and/or other deliverables. Groups often face changes to the problem situations in multiple ways, including changing perspectives, task requirements, or situational variables that have emerged. These curveballs are often challenging for groups; they require students to engage in strategies that allow them to reflect on managing ambiguity and change.

Next, students present their recommended solutions and prepare for feedback, revisions, and often sequels to the project questions and contexts. To conclude this phase, students reflect on their journey and give and receive feedback to themselves, peers, teachers, and any audiences that participated in this work. This is a time for students to reflect on their learning and their performance related to solving the problems, and articulate new questions that emerged from the project for future inquiries.

What students do during this phase:

1. Revisit the entry experience, driving questions, learning intentions, and success criteria to determine key knows/need-to-knows.

2. Engage individually or in small teams to address the driving question by understanding the problem, establishing criteria for a solution, identifying potential solutions, and then selecting a solution.

3. Participate in a number of workshops to sharpen transfer-level skills, including engaging with people directly involved with the problem, exploring themes and patterns in other contexts, and developing strategies to maintain social-emotional well-being.

4. Incorporate curveballs into solutions.

5. Present tentative findings to others and give and receive feedback.

6. Work in small teams to propose solutions and discuss potential applications across contexts.

7. Reflect on performance, progress, and process.

Primary Example
1. Students review the expectations of learning about the development, adoption, and enforcement of rules in their local community.
2. Students spend time scanning multiple contexts in which rules are developed, adopted, and enforced, including classroom context, local community, rural Indigenous communities around the world, representative democracies, and direct democracies.
3. Collectively the students generate one or more driving questions (e.g., *To what extent are laws developed to protect everyone? Where can we improve laws to be fully inclusive of our entire community? Should we change our laws to meet the demands of the 21st century?*).
4. Students form into groups to solve the driving question. Here they learn how to use an analytical or design-based strategy.
5. Teachers provide workshops on scanning multiple situations and how to use metaphors and analogies to better understand similarities and differences between contexts. Questions might include: What are the similarities and differences in how rules are formed, followed, and enforced? What trends and patterns do we see emerging in these situations? Where are there similarities and differences between the context you are studying and the contexts we are reviewing? How does this scanning exercise help you in solving the problem?
6. Additional workshops include learning how to handle challenges (How will we handle setbacks if and when new information emerges? How will we handle group dynamics issues?) and engaging in authentic situations (How do we work with our local community officials? Who should we talk to? How will we listen to them respectfully and gather the information we need?).
7. Each student group is presented with a change in the problem they are working on. For example, one group is tasked with facing a change in a new controversial law in the town and how that will likely be received and enforced. Other students find a law has been revoked and is no longer required to be adhered to. They analyze what responsibilities city officials have on educating the population on these changes and what the most effective strategy may be.
8. Students draft presentations in a TED Talk style, having eight minutes to present their solutions to a problem by using a story to articulate the core theme of their solution. Students receive feedback from peers using the Tuning protocol.
9. Students are tasked with engaging in a sequel to the project by analyzing a new club being developed for youth basketball, and they need to provide recommendations on how to develop, adopt, and enforce rules.
10. Students form new groups and conduct a Think-Pair-Share on their progress, proficiency, and key questions that emerged in the project that remain unanswered. Students also give the teacher feedback on the project and what worked and can be improved in the future.

Table 6.1 Primary Example of Transfer Engagement

Secondary Example

1. Students review the expectations of learning about the implications of corporate monopolies on the economy and the role governments play in regulating corporations. Students spend time scanning multiple contexts where monopolies exist and how governments are regulating them. Students explore their know/need-to-know list as well as their assessment data to determine what else they may need to learn to address the problem(s) they are solving.

2. Students form small groups to solve the driving question. Here they identify a problem-solving process they will use to engage in solving the problem.

3. Teachers offer a workshop on scanning multiple contexts in which monopolies exist. Students scan biological contexts in which monocultures thrive and biodiversity is limited (corn farms), English language arts in which books are banned and everyone reads the same book (*Fahrenheit 451*), and monopolies in context, including a neighborhood lemonade stand, power companies (PG&E), and the context they are reviewing with their group (local transit system).

4. Teachers offer additional workshops to support students in interviewing authentic audiences; reflecting on how the issue matters to the students, their families, and the community; and determining a narrative that will support their future presentation.

5. Other workshops include strategies for incorporating choice in the method of presentation and solutions offered.

6. Students face a curveball, including a change in administration that is pro-business or pro-regulation, and they need to investigate the changes to their solution in light of potential legislation. Other students might face the introduction of a client who wants their services and may be from a corporation that is looking to increase marketing and product reach by minimizing competition. Another client might be a local community leader demanding support for local mom-and-pop stores. Students then determine changes that need to be made in their presentation.

7. Students attend workshops to develop their social and emotional well-being. They reflect on how they are feeling about changes and the demands on their work.

8. Students finalize their presentation and conduct a gallery walk, where audiences attend class and provide feedback on their solutions.

9. Students reflect on the feedback, reflect on their goals, and determine next steps they could take to improve their solution.

10. Students conclude by engaging in a 30-minute sequel in which the teacher gives them a new problem in a different context. Students form a new group and have to determine the similarities and differences between the problem they were solving and the problem they just solved.

Table 6.2 Secondary Example of Transfer Engagement

These steps and processes will require collaboration and critical thinking from students, as well as incorporating new scenarios and problems into their schema. Teachers' role as activators here is important to nudge students in their thinking. In Phase 4, teachers incorporate three key habits, identified in Table 6.3.

Rigorous PBL Teacher Habit	Success Criteria
Habit 10: **Return to transfer** by implementing transfer-level workshops to apply learning in real-world contexts and address curveballs	~ Revisit the entry experience, driving questions, learning intentions, and success criteria to determine key knows/need-to-knows ~ Engage individually or in small teams to address the driving question ~ Implement transfer-level workshop to support student learning in how to apply their learning in real-world contexts, problems, and products ~ Engage students in curveballs (perspective, situation, content)
Habit 11: **Deliver on the challenge** by structuring means for showcasing work and giving/ receiving feedback and engaging students in project sequels	~ Structure means for showcasing work and giving/ receiving feedback to/from others ~ Engage students in project sequels
Habit 12: **Look in the mirror** by conducting reflective protocols on academic growth, meeting cultural expectations, and addressing the driving question	~ Conduct reflective protocols on academic growth, meet cultural expectations, and address the driving question

Table 6.3 Phase 4 Habits and Success Criteria

Habit 10: **Return to transfer** *by implementing transfer-level workshops to apply learning in real-world contexts and address curveballs*

The following habit is designed to support students in transitioning from deep-level learning to preparing for a project presentation. Clarity was paramount when students began the project, and it remains just as crucial as their solutions and products come to fruition. Students need to revisit the overall outcomes of learning and examine the problem(s) they are working to solve, form small teams to work through the problem with a well-established process, and participate in transfer-level workshops to develop the knowledge and skills to meet project demands.

Success Criteria: *Revisit the entry experience, driving questions, learning intentions, and success criteria to determine key knows/need-to-knows*

As students emerge from the deep-learning phase of the project, they should take a few minutes to review the journey so far. They have gone through the following:

※ Project launch

※ Pre-assessment

※ Surface- and deep-learning workshops and associated tasks

※ Two-thirds assessment

This is a time to reflect on their key learning, performance, and what key questions they will carry with them into this transfer-level project. The suggestion here is to have students engage in a Think-Pair-Share using the following prompts:

After reviewing the learning intentions and success criteria . . .

※ To what extent do I know the core content I need to address the driving question?

※ What have I learned that is critical to addressing the project problem?

※ How will I gain the knowledge and skills I need to successfully meet the project demands?

After reviewing the entry event and the K/NTK list . . .

❊ What do I know and need to know to address the driving question?

❊ What would best support me in answering the driving question?

❊ How will I go about answering the need-to-knows?

❊ What are my next steps?

Students should write down their answers to the aforementioned questions and prepare to share them with a partner. During the share portion, each student shares their responses. Using a structured protocol is highly encouraged during the sharing portion. Once students have shared with a partner, student groups share out. Those who are listening write down themes and patterns they are noticing that will be important for future learning.

Once each group shares their answers to the original questions, the teacher facilitates a quick Whip Around of the themes and patterns that emerged in the class. These themes and patterns should be used to construct potential transfer-level workshops.

Success Criteria: *Engage individually or in small teams to address the driving question*

Once students have reviewed where they are in their learning, they need to begin working toward solving the driving question. Throughout the project, students have worked as individuals, pairs, and mixed groups. This is intentional; some of our best thinking requires slow, introspective processing time in isolation, and sometimes innovation manifests in the company of others. The trend of fluid grouping (or pairing) continues in this final phase of the project. Consider forming small, temporary working groups. To leverage the perspective of every learner in the group, follow this suggested model:

❊ Assign roles meant to push thinking.

❊ Agree to norms that will encourage multiple perspectives.

❊ Engage in an analytical or design problem-solving process.

Assign roles meant to push thinking. Group roles also play a key function here—but not necessarily as they are traditionally assigned. Rather than assigning task-based roles ("supply manager," "reporter") that divide work responsibilities, we suggest roles that are centered on the process of learning together and solving problems. The purpose of these types of roles is to promote greater interaction between students in solving a problem and move away from simple distribution of labor. This is less factory floor and more beehive, less hierarchy between students and more Socratic sharing of ideas and power. Yes, it may be necessary to clearly define how many and which students will rush the scissors repository. But above delineating material responsibilities, we want to emphasize learners' responsibility to push one another in their thinking.

To keep learning central in learners' minds, process roles suggest an approach different from that of task roles, which tend to divide labor and potentially isolate students who do more or less of their fair share. Table 6.4 compares roles grounded in process versus those used to distribute tasks.

Process Roles	Task Roles
Process Coach: The role is focused on ensuring the team is following established agreements, checking on needs of the group for potential workshops, and all other related next steps. *Questions guiding this role include:* ~ *Are we following our agreements?* ~ *Are we sticking to our agenda?* ~ *Do we know our next steps?* ~ *Do we know how we will check for our progress?*	**Technology Liaison:** This is an established role for executing all the technology-based components for the project. This often revolves around creating products. It frequently leads to silos in which group members focus on compiling information from other students and working primarily on aesthetics. Students often categorize their work based on job responsibilities. Very little authentic collaboration is required to address novel questions, nuanced information, and nimble responses to changes in the project.

Process Roles	Task Roles
Perspective Coach: This role connects deeply with the process coach and the precision coach. The role is focused on analyzing the various perspectives that are being brought into the conversation. *Questions guiding this role include:* ~ *Are we hearing from everyone?* ~ *And from every viewpoint?*	**Community Relations Coordinator:** This person's primary responsibility is to engage with people outside school. This role may require time outside school hours, placing them in an often unfair situation with peers and competing interests. Moreover, students struggle with translating everything they learned from the original source to team members who are expected to learn and use that information.
Precision Coach: This role focuses on the accuracy of information that is being shared by team members as well as the information they are reviewing. *Questions guiding this role include:* ~ *Do we have the facts right?* ~ *Are these decisions based on our collective understanding?*	**Data Analyst:** This role is primarily responsible for engaging in project research. This person spends a significant amount of time communicating their own learning and that of others to convey information that all members must understand.

Table 6.4 Process and Task Roles

Agree to norms that will encourage multiple perspectives. How we work together is one of the most transferable skills students take with them. We suggest norms that encourage students to push one another in their thinking. The purpose here is to give all learners permission, or to make it normal, to bring their voice to the table and to value the voices of others.

One strategy teachers may use—especially those who work with younger students—is to focus on one or two of these norms at a time. Model it during whole-group discussion and be explicit about which norm is the focus. "Today, I'm going to really stick to the norm of using specific examples. So when you explain your thinking, I might ask you, 'Can you give an example?'" is one way to help students understand what the norm looks like and sounds like.

Furthermore, adhering to a couple of these norms in adult discussions can shape the way people say what's on their minds, rather than leaving with false assumptions or unanswered questions. Try taking "discuss the undiscussable" for a spin with colleagues who are reluctant to say what they're really thinking.

The agreements in Table 6.5 are recommended.

Agreement	Description
State views and ask genuine questions	Speak with conviction of ideas and genuinely listen to others. In one first-grade classroom, the students changed the agreement to "speak like you are right and listen like you are wrong."
Use specific examples and agree on what important words mean	Ensure that everyone understands what people mean when they are using language. Oftentimes people are confused by particular acronyms in one discipline, or an adage or metaphor that may be relevant in one context but unclear in another. Taking time to ensure everyone understands and agrees on important words is helpful for dialogue, discussion, debate, and decision-making.
Explain reasoning and intent	Help peers to understand the rationale for an action or a comment being made. People are curious to know what someone's motives may be and how they may connect, or not connect—and discuss why.
Focus on interests, not positions	Focus on the key outcomes rather than a rigid decision that must be adhered to. Take, for example, one student who insists the group make a poster while another demands that they make a video. These are positions. Both students may have an interest in showcasing sufficient knowledge to meet the success criteria, incorporating artistry, and getting the work done on time. If the group focuses on these shared interests, it may be easier to accept one of the positions or co-construct an entirely new solution.

Agreement	Description
Test assumptions and inferences	Give people the space to check their rationale for making certain comments or decisions. When assumptions or inferences are checked, people are able to find out more to determine whether such assumptions are true and seek out ways to investigate them.
Jointly design next steps	The idea here is that people work together to identify, implement, and inspect solutions to problems.
Discuss the undiscussable	Give permission to bring up ideas, questions, or concerns that would most likely be shared elsewhere if they weren't allowed to vet them as a group. This is in direct contrast with the parking lot (or playground) conversations that so commonly sour group progress after students begin working together.

Table 6.5 Class and Group Agreements

Apply a problem-solving process to the driving question. When temporary work groups have agreed-on norms and process roles, they have a framework for how to work together in a way that is different from simply delegating work. A problem-solving process can help to establish how they'll tackle the driving question. Two processes, the analytical approach and the design approach, are recommended here. Teachers may choose either approach depending on the context of their problem or the needs of their students; both approaches are useful to learn and use and are laid out in Table 6.6. Table 6.6 is included in the online Appendix as well.

Approach	Analytical Approach	Design Approach
Sequence	1. **Mindset:** Learn about the context 2. **Problem Definition:** Define the potential problem 3. **Solution Criteria:** Identify the key aspects of any solution 4. **Possible Solutions:** Brainstorm multiple solutions 5. **Solution Choice:** Select a solution 6. **Implementation and Inspection:** Implement and determine next steps	1. **Empathize:** Learn about who is impacted, and how, in the context 2. **Define:** Sharpen key questions to better define the problem 3. **Ideate:** Brainstorm and create solutions 4. **Prototype:** Build representations of one or more ideas 5. **Test:** Test ideas and gain feedback from "users" (those impacted)
Tools	Structured protocols and activities for each phase 1. **Mindframe:** Review Agreements/Constructivist Listening 2. **Problem Definition:** Fishbone 3. **Solution Criteria:** Focusing Four 4. **Possible Solution:** Carousel Brainstorm 5. **Solution Choice:** Nominal Group Technique 6. **Implementation and Inspection:** Data-Driven Dialogue	Structured protocols and activities for each phase 1. **Empathize:** Empathy Maps 2. **Define:** Peeling the Onion 3. **Ideate:** Yes, and . . . 4. **Prototype:** Storyboard 5. **Test:** Test Capture Grid

Table 6.6 Different Problem-Solving Approaches

Success Criteria: *Implement transfer-level workshops to support student learning in how to apply their learning in real-world contexts, problems, and products*

Earlier in the book, we discussed Hattie and Donoghue's (2016) findings that not all instructional strategies are created equal. When choosing how to bring students nearer their learning goal, it is critical to consider strategies that align to the appropriate level of learning. Workshops that are specifically designed for transfer are uniquely helpful in supporting their work at this point. They will (and should) look and sound different from the foundation building that happens early in a project and the subsequent meaning making that follows. In this chapter, we discuss three types of workshops that are tailored to support students' transfer learning. Application, activation, and authenticity workshops (Table 6.7) are ways to structure transfer-level learning based on students' knows/need-to-knows.

Workshop Type 1: **Application** of content and solutions across contexts	Workshop Type 2: **Activation** of strategies to handle transition and ambiguity	Workshop Type 3: **Authenticity** of the choice, context, and content
~ Generating and testing hypotheses ~ Developing analogies and metaphors ~ Comparing contexts using deep-learning strategies	~ Understanding and controlling oneself ~ Understanding and interacting with others	~ Using strategies that are aligned to context of the problem(s) ~ Engaging with people within the context of the problem(s) ~ Analyzing and using contextual and content-based information to solve problems

Table 6.7 Transfer Teaching and Learning Strategies

Another way to frame transfer-level workshops is to think of these three approaches like a lemon:

Application: Lemons to limes. How is the problem we've studied like another problem that occurs? How is it different?

Activation: The bitter pith. What do we do when we encounter the unexpected?

Authenticity: Lemonade stands for change. How do we apply what we know to affect something that is important to us?

Workshop Type 1: Application-Based Workshops

Application skills help learners deliberately apply their skills across situations. Apples to oranges is somewhat analogous, but as this is an opportunity for students to explore subtlety, lemons to limes is more like it. These skills are developed through using strategies that look similar to what students do as they develop deep knowledge. Analogies and Venn diagrams, for example, are relevant for developing the skills to apply across situations. The key difference is how we use these tools in each level of learning. In deep learning, students are comparing and contrasting ideas within a discipline. For example, in the book *Land of the Cranes*, how are the characters of Betita and Marisel similar and different? In transfer situations, students are relating ideas across contexts. Instead of comparing two characters in *Land of the Cranes*, students may compare the dynamic between characters in *Land of the Cranes* to that between the characters in another book, such as *The Outsiders*. Or they may draw comparisons between the fictional activist Marisel and the real-life activist Dolores Huerta.

Application strategies are meant to help learners increase the breadth of what they understand. Three application-based strategies are discussed in Tables 6.8, 6.9, and 6.10.

Application Strategy: Generating Hypotheses	
Key question: Given what we know about _____, what would we do if _____?	
Workshop Process	Students are presented with a local problem of identifying an increase of the COVID-19 virus in wastewater. Public health is cautiously optimistic that this slight increase is nothing to be alarmed by and is likely residual from an outbreak that occurred over a break. Community groups, however, are scared by this data and want city council members to respond with intense masking mandates immediately.
	Students form into small work groups and use the Five Whys protocol to determine the root cause of the problem. During this activity, they ask for additional information they need. Some information is readily available; other information is missing.
	Students begin scenario planning using a chosen protocol and form a set of hypotheses. They share how they would test those hypotheses and recommendations to take immediately and how they will report their learning over time.
	Students repeat this process with what they have been studying about local watersheds. If there is increased fertilizer runoff found in local streams, how could they apply similar methods to determine if it is due to a one time event or a more endemic problem that should be addressed by the county agricultural commissioner?
Example	Provide students with a problem that is different from the one they are solving. Ask them to . . .
	1. Determine the underlying problem(s).
	2. Discuss the key information you need to address the problem.
	3. Make a guess on what you think will be required to have a satisfactory solution.
	4. Form a number of hypotheses. What would happen if (a) no intervention occurs, (b) you engage in your plan and it doesn't work, or (c) you engage in your plan and it works?
	5. Draft a list of ways that you would test if your hypotheses were right or wrong.
	6. Repeat the same process with the problem at hand.

Application Strategy: Generating Hypotheses	
Key question: Given what we know about _____, what would we do if _____?	
Toolbox	The following tools are helpful to support students in generating ideas, making predictions, and testing hunches: ~ Explanation Game ~ Think, Puzzle, Explore ~ Imagine If . . . ~ Chalk Talk

Table 6.8 Generating Hypotheses Strategy Description

Application Strategy: Developing Analogies and Metaphors	
Key questions: How is this problem like another problem? How is it different?	
Workshop Process	1. Provide students with one context. 2. Ask students to generate a situation that is analogous/metaphorical to that context. 3. Ask students to share their contexts with others and discuss how the analogous/metaphorical situation is similar or different. 4. Place students in small groups and ask them to look at the analogous situations in the following way: *How does your analogy or metaphor compare to core ideas and solutions to problems?* 5. Ask groups to generate additional analogous situations in different contexts. What are other contexts that relate to the situations you have generated? What themes and patterns do you notice in books, movies, articles, and life experiences that appear to have some connection to the problems we are already working on?
Example	Students are shown an example of a feedback loop in which prices of toilet paper fell because of a decline in demand. Students are tasked with creating analogous situations.

Application Strategy: Developing Analogies and Metaphors *Key questions: How is this problem like another problem? How is it different?*	
Toolbox	The following tools are helpful to support students in developing analogies and metaphors: ~ 3-2-1 Bridge ~ Creative Comparisons ~ Options Explosions ~ Parts, Purposes, and Complexities

Table 6.9 Analogies and Metaphors Strategy Description

Application Strategy: Comparing Contexts Using Deep-Learning Strategies *Key questions: What are the subtle differences between contexts? Why is that important?*	
Workshop Process	1. Provide students with two or more contexts. 2. Ask students to use a Venn diagram and write down the similarities and differences between each context. 3. Ask students to share their Venn diagrams and compare and contrast what they wrote. In small groups, students should answer the following questions: *What do our Venn diagrams have in common? What is different?* 4. Ask students to answer follow-up questions, including the following: *What subtle differences do you notice in the problem situation? What are subtle similarities between these problems?* 5. Ask students to relate their Venn diagrams to their current problems. *How are they similar and different?* 6. Students address the following question and share out: *How could comparing and contrasting across contexts be helpful in understanding a problem and forming a solution?*

Application Strategy: Comparing Contexts Using Deep-Learning Strategies *Key questions: What are the subtle differences between contexts? Why is that important?*	
Example	Students compare Picasso's painting *Guernica* and a mural created during the Black Lives Matter movement. Students are asked to compare and contrast both and identify the similarities and differences between the historical and social contexts that inspired the painting and mural.
Toolbox	The following tools are helpful to support students in comparing and contrasting: ~ +1 Routine ~ Generate-Sort-Connect-Elaborate ~ Portable Surprise ~ Headlines

Table 6.10 Comparing Contexts Strategy Description

Many of the tools listed above come from Project Zero of the Harvard Graduate School of Education.

Workshop Type 2: Activation-Based Workshops

Activation workshops are designed to help learners work through the bitter pith of unexpected problems. When solutions seem out of reach or relationships need to be restored or maintained, activation strategies are important. These strategies are especially relevant when students engage in the following:

❊ Working in small groups – handling self and social dynamics

❊ Addressing curveballs – negotiating setbacks and ambiguous situations

❊ Engaging with authentic audiences – working with novel perspectives, respecting differences, and engaging in thoughtful dialogue and reflective listening

❊ Presenting – navigating stressful performance-based situations

❊ Reflecting on the process – analyzing emotional well-being and ability to handle uncomfortable situations

Students are often confronted with "cognitive emotions"—an emotional response when something we thought followed a familiar pattern or routine turns out to be more challenging. This can happen nearly anywhere: when writing a narrative, adding new steps to mathematical procedures, or grappling with ideologies that challenge how you make sense of the world. In this way, learners in all stages of life share common ground. We seek comfort and joy, and we steer clear of what vexes us. When considering the cognitive emotions that arise during learning, Claxton (2021) shares that the following questions often permeate the conscious minds of students:

❋ Where did this come from?

❋ How can I make that (good thing) happen again?

❋ How can I avoid or neutralize that (bad thing)?

Claxton (2021) further states that "surprise is what throws us, what doesn't conform to our existing picture of the world, and it is therefore especially significant for our survival and flourishing" (p. 74). All in all, the aforementioned experiences involve sharing power with others, reflecting on handling setbacks, and developing strategies to navigate ambiguity and setbacks. Table 6.11 illustrates a number of strategies that support students in taking an active role in developing their emotional intelligence.

Activation Strategy: Self-Awareness and Self-Management Key question: What is the story I'm telling myself?	
Purpose	The following protocols enhance students' ability to understand their motives, the stories (i.e., inferences) they are telling themselves, the emotions that come from those stories, and the actions they take from those stories and emotions. Students need strategies to check their motives and stories and devise other strategies to best manage emotions and take more effective actions.

Activation Strategy: Self-Awareness and Self-Management Key question: What is the story I'm telling myself?	
Example	Before writing arguments for or against increasing the minimum wage, students pair off to state their claims and ask one another, "What makes you say that?" Partners take notes to document their peer's response and ask again and again to help their classmate identify the roots of their emotional connection to their claim.
Toolbox	~ What Makes You Say That? ~ Claim, Support, Question ~ Think, Puzzle, Explore ~ Who Am I?

Table 6.11 Self-Awareness and Self-Management Strategy Description

Activation Strategy: Social Awareness and Social Management Key question: What is the story other people are telling?	
Purpose	The following protocols support students in managing the motives, stories, and emotions of the entire group or team. The following protocols enable students to establish agreements to keep people psychologically safe, ensure we check perspectives, and take actions that promote healthy relationships in times of change and challenge.
Example	Students have been asked to rewrite a well-known myth with twists to the plot, character, or setting that impact the overall theme. When group members disagree about which myth they will choose to retell, they meet with the teacher, and each side adopts the other's viewpoint in a Circle of Viewpoints protocol. The teacher or a peer mediator then helps the group discuss what they learned from taking on the viewpoint of someone else in their group, and guides the team to a final decision.
Toolbox	~ Step In–Step Out–Step Back ~ Circles of Action ~ Circle of Viewpoints ~ Feelings and Options

Table 6.12 Social Awareness and Social Management Strategy Description

The workshops laid out in Table 6.12 are often employed with small groups as opposed to the entire class. As such, teachers often post on the whiteboard optional workshops that students can attend, or they set up rotational workshops that groups attend.

Teachers may also engage in 1:1 meetings or ask specific group members who are serving in one of the process roles to attend a workshop. For example, the teacher may ask for all students who are process coaches to meet and discuss social awareness via a structured workshop.

Workshop Type 3: Authenticity-Based Workshops

Authenticity workshops ask the question "To what extent can I apply this to something important to me?" If we are experts on lemons, how could we create a lemonade stand for the common good? Authenticity skills are associated with the following questions:

✳ To what extent does the following problem or situation authentically align with the core discipline(s) under study?

✳ To what extent does the following problem or situation authentically align with the actual context of the problem?

✳ To what extent do students get to authentically create and solve the problem or situation at hand?

As such, authenticity is built on the degree to which what students are learning resembles the world outside school. It involves the content students are studying, the context in which they are working to solve a problem, and the choices that students have in solving the problem.

Content: *Academic knowledge and skills that are used in the real world.* Research continues to show that the ability to engage in real-world tasks and apply learning requires core content knowledge within the actual real-world situation. To promote the development of core content as a means of increasing authenticity, students should consider the following key questions: To what extent does the task and context relate to the content area (discipline) I'm learning about? To what extent do I need to learn surface and deep knowledge in one or more disciplines to work through the authentic challenges I'm working on?

Aspect of Authenticity: Content **Key question: How does this apply to a real-world problem?**	
Process	Students are tasked with determining the success criteria they have met so far in the project. They bring any and all assessment data to the workshop. Next, students discuss what they know and how it relates to the problem(s) they are working on (via discussion mapping). Students then identify what they don't know and why this may be important to address the problem. They discuss potential next steps.
Example	Students come together to discuss what they know so far in their current social studies and language arts unit, in which they're meant to create a book for visitors that describes the most important ways their community has changed over time. They bring exit tickets, graphic organizers, maps, and drafts of their writing. Through their discussion, it becomes clear that there are two key words ("indigenous" and "basin") that many students still don't completely understand. They are, however, able to relate previous thoroughfares and housing areas to current ones. It also becomes clear that the class agrees on four of the most important changes in their community but are unsure what the fifth one should be. The class determines that they need a brief review of the key terms they are struggling with, as well as one more learning block to analyze photos of their town during its major flood in the 1970s. The teacher maps the class discussion and shows students the results after they conclude.
Toolbox	~ Discussion mapping ~ Gap Analysis ~ Fishbone

Table 6.13 Authenticity Content-Based Strategy Description

Context: *Contemporaneous real-world situations, opportunities, challenges, and people.* Students are drawn to problems of the present and problems that connect to them in some way. Knowledge needs to be connected to personal histories and current concerns, if it is to "empower" anyone to get things done that matter to them (Claxton, 2021, p. 52). Students are buzzing with questions: What is happening now? How does that connect to me, my family, and my friends? How can I take part in solving that problem? Such questions are all powerful motivators for students.

In traditional PBL experiences, students are gearing up to present to high-stakes audiences. For example, students may be expected to present a proposal for a new marketing strategy to a panel of businesspeople. While this quasi—*Shark Tank* approach has its uses, we suggest spending more time providing students with expert advisers throughout the inquiry process. This gives students the opportunity to engage more naturally and more formatively with adults outside the classroom. In addition, in a very practical sense, it opens up the calendar to have professionals visit and offer input when it works for their schedules, rather than making the crux of adult–student interaction rest on one nonnegotiable performance date. Our experience is that inviting professionals to Zoom in or stop by for a class visit while the work is still in development benefits student learning and better mimics the real world.

Furthermore, incorporating expert advisers can broaden students' thinking about applying their skills in different contexts. Take, for example, a situation where high-quality writing revisions are a part of students' success criteria. The number of professionals who revise their writing is vast. Marketing professionals, journalists, public relations specialists, and people who must present or write to a large audience probably make revisions on a regular basis. Inviting adults—in person or virtually—who can answer questions about their process with students can help add relevance and increase the quality of students' work in a way that is realistic for teachers to organize. We need students to see the act of contribution to be part of our daily experience, not only high-stakes summative projects.

Aspect of Authenticity: Context Key question: How does this relate to what's happening right now?	
Process	Students engage in two contextual workshops: (1) How does this connect to me? and (2) Where does this impact others? In each workshop, students engage in the following process: 1. Brainstorm collectively (e.g., Carousel Brainstorm) to answer aforementioned questions. 2. Discuss (with peers and outside experts). 3. Develop a plan (with peers and outside experts). 4. Present for feedback—what is my story, their story, our story? How do we incorporate this framing into our understanding of the problem as well as how we engage in solving the problem and presenting the problem solution?
Example	Students are learning to apply slope-intercept form as they produce line graphs. The class engages in a Carousel Brainstorm in which they brainstorm ways that seeing a steady increase or decrease, as represented in a graph, could be important to them or to others. Ideas that are generated include the price of collector sneakers over time, a reduction in one's speed running the mile in phys-ed class, and a decrease in the number of Fudgsicles in the local ice cream truck. Students develop a plan to create their own word problems for a teen audience as well as an audience of little kids, in which a line graph could help buyers make a decision. Throughout the process, they are engaging with multiple stakeholders.
Toolbox	~ Carousel Brainstorm ~ Three Stories

Table 6.14 Authenticity Context-Based Strategy Description

Choice: *Autonomy within the confines of an authentic context.* Students need a level of defined autonomy in the class. Clear boundaries surrounding a set of choices for students could include which specific question(s) to work on, the products to create, the choice of group members to work with, and choice of problem-solving strategies. The following questions are helpful to prime such discussions:

Who can I engage with to learn about various perspectives and potential people and organizations that I may be able to work with over the course of study? Where do I have an opportunity to express my perspective on the product/presentation/process/work structure (group)? To what extent do I have a choice in how I display my work? Where are the boundaries of my choice?

Aspect of Authenticity: Choice Key question: Where do I have autonomy and freedom within this project?	
Process	Share with students broad parameters of task, and ask students to select a means for presenting their solution. In addition, how will they gain the requisite skills to engage in that product? Provide the team with 10 minutes to discuss their ideas with their team and prepare a plan. Next, have groups meet with one other group to share their ideas with others and receive informal feedback using a protocol (e.g., Tuning protocol). Consider repeating the process, discussing how individual perspective is included in the project/process.
Example	Students are tasked with informing their community about the benefits of different produce sold at their farmers' market. Their products need to describe three ways the fruit or vegetable benefits the human body (e.g. vitamin C) and/or the environment (e.g. low water usage). Students can choose to share their information via podcast, poster, video recording, or another medium that meets the success criteria. Groups are given 10 minutes and a simple graphic organizer to prepare a plan. Then, each group shares with another group and gives/receives specific feedback through the Tuning protocol. Each group makes changes to their plan based on feedback and submits their idea to the teacher for approval before moving forward.
Toolbox	~ Tuning protocol ~ TAG protocol

Table 6.15 Authenticity Choice-Based Strategy Description

Success Criteria: *Engage students in curveballs*

Curiosity—the desire to engage and explore—is often piqued by our interests and passions but is also ignited by surprise and all its variations: confusion, frustration, disappointment, delight, and shock. —(Claxton, 2021, p. 71)

"Somebody wanted, but, so then" is a simple phrase teachers have used for years to help students retell stories. The phrase works because it captures the conflict and resolution of nearly any plot. It also sounds right for what we encounter in the world outside school walls. "I planned to be a flight attendant, but there was a hiring freeze, so I taught English abroad instead. Then I found a way to travel and get paid for something I loved." For teachers who have sat on panels for senior-year presentations, this phrasing is ubiquitous too. At student presentations, even if it's not intentional, it's common to hear seniors explain what they had *planned* to do and what they had to change because of circumstances out of their control. "I wanted to design a set with the local theater, but their show was already in rehearsals, so I had to paint a set instead. Then my public presentation changed to the backdrop I detailed." In life, change is bound to happen. Curveballs are more the rule than the exception. One way to help students transfer what they know is to make a habit of throwing them curveballs.

As students and teachers prepare to move toward the final phase of the rigorous PBL process, they need to experience the fluid nature of real problems. They also are going to need to be clear on learning expectations and be able to discern the context of the project from the content they are learning. One way to do this is by incorporating small changes into the project context. These changes, or curveballs, present students with new contextual information that requires them to ensure they know what they need to do and prepare for contextual variables.

Let's look at an example of a curveball (see Table 6.16). In the following video example, students are applying their knowledge of geography to a situation outside school: they're advising families where to travel for a vacation. As students finalize their recommendations, their teacher shows them a video of travel restrictions being enforced because of an outbreak of COVID-19. Unfortunately, students who were recommending any towns or parks in that area have to change their plans. They still need to rely on their understanding of distance, environment, and travel routes, but their recommendations must change. The curveball has been pitched.

Steps to Address the Curveball

1. Assess student readiness for a curveball (do they have a thorough understanding of core content and the overall problem they are attempting to solve?).

2. Prepare students by sharing that we are about to receive news that will likely require us to change our plans for solving the problem.

3. Introduce the curveball.

4. Provide students a few minutes to process and discuss the changes (questions should explore what stays the same, what is different, and what next steps they likely need to consider).

5. Ask students what support they may need to address the change and prepare for the presentation or deliverable.

Table 6.16 Curveball Example

There are many types of curveballs for students to consider. The recommendation here is to present students with one of the following changes in Table 6.17. Share with them that this information will likely impact the overall project solutions. Let students know they will have time to inspect the change, evaluate the similarities and differences between the new change and preexisting conditions, and be asked to determine what content becomes critical to solving the problem.

Type of Curveball	Description	Example	Tools
Task Expectations	The product or the presentation students are working on has new specifications.	A vendor is unable to attend your presentation and would like a three-page summary of your plan instead. The marketing team has reviewed your slide deck and would like you to create a brief podcast on your proposal.	~ Generate-Sort-Connect-Elaborate ~ Same and Different
Perspective Change	The students are tasked with understanding multiple perspectives within a problem context and how to incorporate those perspectives into the problem-based situation.	An antitax group wants to share their perspective on your plan to expand funds for paving local roads.	~ Circle of Viewpoints ~ Tug for Truth ~ True for Who?

Type of Curveball	Description	Example	Tools
Situational Change	Students face a change in the conditions of the context they are working in and must identify what and how they must change in their understanding of the problem and potentially their solution to the problem.	Students find out the strategy they were considering may be impacted by supply chain issues.	~ Options Diamonds ~ Options Explosions ~ Generate-Sort-Connect-Elaborate
Cross-Context Problem	Students are faced with working on a new problem in a different context and are tasked with identifying what they can apply from their earlier problem to this new situation.	Students had been designing a floor plan for an arcade, but now they are asked to be consultants for floor plans in a restaurant.	~ Same and Different ~ Generate-Sort-Connect-Elaborate ~ Projecting across Distance

Table 6.17 Curveball Descriptions and Strategies

To support students in addressing a curveball, the following steps are recommended:

1. Use protocols to process the curveball.

2. Use a K/NTK list to plot out expected learning and to develop a plan of action.

3. To address key questions, provide a workshop on application, activation, or authenticity.

a. Application-based workshops would be associated with questions like: Where does this happen elsewhere, and how have others solved these problems? To what extent does that learning apply in this context? What nuances can I incorporate from my learning elsewhere to apply here?

b. Activation-based workshops would be associated with self- and social awareness and management. Questions associated with these workshops include: To what extent am I using tools to effectively handle ambiguity in my learning? Where can I improve in my overall self-management and regulation?

c. Authenticity-based workshops would be helpful if the following questions emerge: Where do I have autonomy? How does this curveball link to the overall learning in this project? Who do I need to listen to to better understand the dynamics of the changes presented in this curveball and how to best address it?

For those just starting out:

If you are engaging in this habit for the first time, keep it manageable. Engage in small changes and select only a few students to participate at first.

Well versed:

If this is a habit you have already established in your classroom, then try presenting several changes to different groups of students and have them share their recommendations to each other. Gallery walls are a wonderful way to showcase the work of others.

Another option is to offer a sequel to a few student groups. These groups are called Skunk Works groups and essentially solve an entirely unique problem. Skunk Works is particularly fun for those student groups who finish early and can be given creative space and autonomy to innovate while the teacher supports those groups who need more adult support.

Habit 11: **Deliver on the challenge** *by structuring means for showcasing work and giving/receiving feedback and engaging students in project sequels*

A hallmark of traditional PBL is that it culminates in a presentation for peers, teachers, or a community audience. Besides giving students valuable experience honing their presentation skills, this process often results in students adding extra polish to their finished product. When there is someone beyond their teacher to witness their efforts, learners tend to elevate the quality of their work.

One critical aspect to add to this "inquire, learn, present" model, however, is the importance of interaction. Think of press conferences, board meetings, and vendor exhibitions. Rarely is a presenter given the luxury of gesturing to their slides and reading off carefully prepared note cards without some sort of questioning from the intended audience. This type of questioning requires that presenters think critically and creatively about what they know.

Presentations outside school often involve interruptions, back-and-forth dialogue, just-in-time feedback, and in-the-moment discussion of potential next steps and questions that need to be answered. Moreover, they often lead to presenters (or students) applying their transfer skills to a new question or new context. This creates a relevant need for learners to pursue a sequel. What better way to ensure that students can apply their learning to more than one context than to regularly make that part of the journey?

Success Criteria: *Structure means for showcasing work and giving/receiving feedback to/from others*

To create an environment where presentations are authentically interactive, teachers can consider a variety of formats. Some ideas include the following:

⁕ TED Talk – Students present without interruptions, and Q&A/feedback follows in sequence.

✳ Workshop – Students engage in multiple presentations simultaneously, and the small audience for each group interacts with students. The audience asks questions, participates in activities, and offers feedback as they enter different group presentations.

✳ Sales Pitch – Students provide a brief presentation, followed by a number of questions and potential feedback related to the needs of a customer.

✳ Situation Room – Students are presented with a briefing related to their project and must offer recommendations as well as adapt recommendations to incoming information.

Resist the temptation to fall back on group presentations as usual. Help students to develop the habit of expecting a discourse to result from what they present, as well as the expectation that their learning and thinking is not done just because the last note card reads, "This concludes . . ." Ensure that presentation structures include (1) an input session, (2) a feedback session, and (3) next steps.

Presentation Cycle	Input Session	Feedback Session	Next Steps
Steps	1. Students prepare their materials for the audience 2. Students present core content	1. Students use tools to capture feedback (such as whiteboards, sticky notes, or a digital document) 2. Audience provides feedback using a structured protocol	1. Students share their next steps in relation to the feedback 2. Students listen to others' next steps 3. Students refine their own steps and proceed

Presentation Cycle	Input Session	Feedback Session	Next Steps
Recommended Tools	~ Gallery walk ~ World Café ~ TEDx presentation	~ Critical Friends ~ Tuning protocol ~ Learning Dilemma	~ Concentric Circles ~ Think-Pair-Share ~ Fishbowl

Table 6.18 Presentation Strategies

Success Criteria: *Engage students in project sequels*

At the conclusion of a project, students should have an opportunity to evaluate the context they are studying with a completely new situation. This is not a time to solve a new problem but rather a time to spot the differences between another situation and stimulate continued transfer learning.

Two sequel examples and the process are outlined in Table 16.19.

Learning	Original context	Sequel
Volume	Studying volume by determining the time it would take to fill up a pool with soda	Studying volume and determining how much water would be needed to sink a boat, as well as the time it would take to sink a boat with a leak in the hull
Leadership	Writing an essay about how U.S. presidents have handled U.S.—Russia relations involving Ukraine	Conducting an oral presentation on restaurants' leadership as the establishments transition away from Covid safety measures

Table 6.19 Spot the Difference

This entire activity should take less than 20 minutes and is truly a wonderful way to stimulate, assess, and provide feedback on student transfer.

Practitioner's Note: *Always design and implement from the place of "Now what?"*

> **Key Message:** Transfer learning is not merely an academic exercise but an opportunity for students to contribute to making the world a better place.

We are wired to contribute, to take meaningful action. In the book *The Knowledge Illusion: The Myth of Individual Thought and the Power of Collective Wisdom*, Sloman and Fenbach (2017) share that "thought is for action. Thinking [and explicit knowing] evolved as an extension of the ability to act effectively; [they] evolved to make us better at doing what's necessary to achieve our goals" (pp. 10–11). Humanity's highest goals boil down to doing things with and for others. If that is the case, then transfer learning—and, for that matter, rigorous learning—can't be accomplished in isolation of service. A contribution to the greater good is a requisite to developing rigorous learning.

How can we best ensure that contribution is a part of the DNA of our work in transfer? How do we support students in approaching all problems as an act of contribution?

Design questions for "Now what?"

The more we can center our driving questions on the ethos that we are always trying to be better people and make the world a better place, the higher likelihood that we are designing problems and projects that are both meaningful and cognitively demanding.

One way that is helpful to design questions for contribution is through a simple process. One suggested process is by following these three steps:

Step One: The first step is related to the outcomes of the discipline. Start with the driving question as it is currently drafted. For example, the question may be How do the results of World War II impact today's world?

Step Two: The second step is related to the relevance of the outcome of the discipline. Identify the purpose for asking this question to today's students. For instance, you may want to ask yourself: So what does this question do to improve my life and make the world a better place? In the previous example, we may change the question to, How does studying World War II give us insight into preventing another war?

Step Three: The third step is related to the contributions students can make from the outcomes of the discipline. Here you want to ask Now what do we do right now to improve my life and the life of others to make the world a better place. In the previous example the question could be changed to: To what extent can we take action to prevent another war?

Approach all problems from a point of criticality.

Gholdi Muhammad defines *criticality* in the following way:

> Criticality is the capacity and ability to read, write, think, and speak in ways to understand power and equity in order to understand and promote anti-oppression. I define oppression simply as any wrongdoing, hurt, or harm. . . . As long as oppression is present, students need spaces to name, interrogate, resist, agitate, and work toward social change. This will support students toward being critical consumers and producers of information. It will also help to build a better humanity for all. With each lesson or unit plan, teachers should ask, *How does our curriculum and instruction help us understand power, equity, and anti-oppression?* (Ferlazzo, 2020)

When we think about designing and implementing transfer work, we need to use the power of "Now what? to bring critical thinking (analytical thinking) and criticality (power, equity, and anti-oppression) into action. During Phase 3 and Phase 4 of a rigorous project, we need to push the curveballs from simply intellectual exercises to "Now what do we do with this new learning?"

One way to move criticality into action is to incorporate the following prompts into our inquiry with students:

※ Now that you see this issue from multiple perspectives, what actions are you compelled to take in your life and in order to advocate for others?

※ To what extent do we better understand the perspectives and insights of others? How will that influence our solutions to a problem?

※ Who do we need to speak with to better understand the situation(s) we are engaging in?

※ What "truths" have we taken for granted? How will we use such learning to improve our understanding and actions? How will we break past patterns?

Approach all problems from a point of valuing student communication.

Student voice is beyond important in learning and simply critical to contributing to real-world problems. To ensure student voice is valued in both quantity and quality, three actions should be considered:

※ Use protocols that ensure our utmost respect for student voice.

 a. Feedback protocols (Critical Friends, Tuning)

 b. Discussion protocols (discussion mapping, Socratic seminar)

 c. Reading, writing, and talking tasks (Four A's, Final Word)

※ Set time for students to engage in discussions with people outside the school.

 a. Schedule interviews via Zoom or a field trip or with in-class visitors who are connected to the problem(s) students are working on.

    b.   Provide time for students to engage in focus groups and interviews and reflect on surveys with people from outside the school.

❊   Design tasks that are aligned with current problems in the real world. Task students with presenting in venues where these problems are being tackled.

    a.   Center student deliverables (e.g., presentations) on real-world venues that are working on the problem (e.g., students present at a board meeting or staff meeting to pitch a solution to a nonprofit).

    b.   Connect student work to problems that are actually being worked on in your community or around the world. Connect students to people working on the problem and find a way for students to offer solutions to the problem.

Habit 12: **Look in the mirror** *by conducting reflective protocols on academic growth, meeting cultural expectations, and addressing the driving question*

The final action habit is focused on student and staff reflections. Students engage in protocols that focus their reflections on their own performance, the quality of the project, and support from both peers and the teacher, along with additional questions that emerged throughout the project. Here, a few simple, well-understood protocols are used that effectively end the project and prepare for the next unit of study.

Success Criteria: *Conduct reflective protocols on academic growth, meet cultural expectations, and address the driving question*

Similar to the beginning of the phase, students should reflect on their performance, key learning, and key questions that still remain. In addition, this is a time for students to give feedback to the teacher and next steps to improve both the project and future work. Protocols to structure these conversations are recommended and include the following:

❋   What? So What? Now What?

❋   Concentric Circles

❋   Think-Pair-Share

❋   Fishbowl

The final student action should be to review the K/NTK list, determine additional questions they have regarding the project, and forecast next steps they would take if they were to continue the project. Modeling the ongoing inquiry process and illustrating the iterative nature of our work—and that we never arrive—is a powerful experience for students.

Conclusion

Similar to Phase 1, students and teachers are engaging in transfer-level work. Phase 4 has multiple steps and a significant number of habits that are often new to teachers who are engaging in this methodology for the first time or are moving away from other, less impactful, forms of problem or project-based learning.

Review Questions

❋   What are the steps you can take to "return to transfer" with students? When looking at Habit 10, which success criteria seems to be doable right now to implement and impact student learning?

❋   What are the steps you can take to "deliver on the challenge" with students? When looking at Habit 11, which success criteria seems to be doable right now to implement and impact student learning?

❋   What are steps you can take to "look in the mirror" with students? When looking at Habit 12, which success criteria seems to be doable right now to implement and impact student learning?

✳ How could you layer new habits into your preexisting habits (e.g., set plays, stacking; see Chapter 7 for additional information on developing, implementing, and sustaining habits)?

Next Steps

✳ Select one of the three habits to incorporate into your daily lessons. Determine whether this habit will occur prior to what you are already doing or after your current practice.

✳ Create a set play for one of the habits and find a way to be held accountable for engaging in the habit over time (see Chapter 7 for more information).

Chapter 7

INSPECTING OUR IMPACT

> **"** The more you learn, the harder it gets. The better you get, the worse you are—because the flaws that you wouldn't even think of looking at before are now visible and need to be addressed. If you want to grow, if you want to progress, you need to always dig deeper.
>
> —Maria Konnikova

In her book *The Biggest Bluff: How I Learned to Pay Attention, Master Myself, and Win,* psychologist Maria Konnikova explores what it takes to develop actionable habits to improve a craft. Using her own money, she meticulously builds the habits necessary to be successful at high-stakes poker. She argues that one of the greatest gifts of poker is that it fights against the greatest of delusions—overconfidence. We may bask in our plans, our strategy, our new learning, but experience has a way of illuminating the imperfections of our ideas and opportunities for growth.

Is developing skills at poker analogous to teaching? Maybe it should be. Formative assessment, when done right, counters the delusion of overconfidence. When we use the evidence yielded by assessments in a formative manner, no matter how certain we were about our own effectiveness, we find out how the cards are truly dealt. We see which students are lost, which are bored, and which are right with us. This provides us with a sober appraisal of our actions and an opportunity to respond. This chapter focuses on how we can use evidence to celebrate, improve, and innovate our habits over time and, as a result, improve student learning and improve contemporary learning with our colleagues.

We argue this is accomplished by engaging in the following habits:

- ❋ **Make discourse deliberate.** While positive relationships alone do not cause effective instruction, they are certainly necessary to ensure we make an impact on student learning. We need to ensure we structure conversations that build positive relationships and hold teams accountable for growing in their habit development and making an improvement in student outcomes.

- ❋ **Sprint.** Teachers are time poor; it's most realistic to make a small change in practice, test that practice with a small group of students, and do so in a short duration of time. As such, teachers need to engage in rapid improvement processes. Learning sprints are recommended here.

- ❋ **Choose action.** Part of an impactful and innovative culture is choosing actions that deliberately improve on practices and also deliberately deviate from current practice to stretch our practices and student learning. Therefore, educators must lower the challenges of bringing in, eliminating, or improving on habits.

Rigorous PBL Teacher Design Habit	Success Criteria
Habit 13: **Make discourse deliberate** by agreeing to shared values and behaviors for shared work and following through on them	~ Agree to shared values and assumptions and behaviors for shared work ~ Follow through on shared values, assumptions, and behaviors
Habit 14: **Sprint** by adhering to a rapid improvement process	~ Adhere to a rapid improvement process
Habit 15: **Choose action** by implementing a personalized plan for improving habits	~ Implement a personalized plan for improving habits ~ Incorporate deliberate deviations in practice

Table 7.1 Inspection Habits Overview

Habit 13: **Make discourse deliberate** *by agreeing to shared values and behaviors for shared work and following through on them*

How we talk to each other is important. What we talk about is important too. The option to shy away from a critical look at student learning can easily become a default. After all, in school, there are so many other things to talk about. Bell schedules, bus duty in the rain, delayed parent conferences, and "Did you get to this part of the unit yet?" are always going to vie for the airspace between teachers. Talking directly about our impact with one another takes deliberate effort. Sustaining that discourse in a way that maintains positive relationships among one another requires a shared understanding of how to engage. One important habit that moves us toward an answer is to structure our conversations in a way that blends both emotional safety and a bias toward action. The following conversational criteria is recommended to move toward such ends.

Success Criteria: *Agree to shared values and behaviors for shared work.*

Just as "we do" amplifies student voice and agency in the classroom, mutual learning among teachers is the rule here. It is not on one teacher to run the show, nor for all teachers to keep their own learning and teaching private. Teachers work hand in hand with each other to learn about their impact on student learning, the use of action-based habits, and tentative next steps. A deliberate discourse about impact can foster creativity, inspiration, and shared support. All the same, it is easy to fall back into unspoken norms of "be nice" or "do just enough to get by." Agreeing to shared values and behaviors—and following through on those agreements—can make it easier to converse with honesty and professional respect.

Figure 7.1 illustrates the key values, assumptions, behaviors, and results of a culture of shared responsibility of learning. This figure is based on the work of Roger Schwarz, Chris Argyris, and Don Schön.

Success Criteria: *Follow through on shared values, assumptions, and behaviors*

This success criteria is met through the following steps.

Step 1: Use operating norms in daily action

The norms in Figure 7.1 provide teams with the types of behaviors that allow them to effectively manage change and hold each other accountable. It's one thing to put them on a poster or in an agenda; it's another thing to put them to work for the purpose of mutual learning. These norms must be embedded in routine language. For example, a teacher may say, "I want to test an assumption that all students were unable to give each other accurate feedback." Or, "When you shared that we should all focus on clarity, it was obvious this was really important to you. I want to better understand where this comes from. Would you explain your reasoning?" Or, "It appears that we all disagree on what direction we should go. Could we step back and refocus on our real interest here and see if we come up with a different way forward?"

Mutual learning values:

Transparency

Curiosity

Informed choice

Accountability

Compassion

Opportunities for learning

Mutual learning assumptions:

I have information, and so do other people

People may disagree with me and still have pure motives

I may be contributing to the problem

Each of us sees things others don't

Differences are opportunities for learning

Acts like

Behaviors:

State views and ask genuine questions

Share all revelant information

Use specific examples and agree on what important words mean

Explain reasoning and intent

Focus on interest, not positions

Test assumptions and inferences

Jointly design next steps

Discuss undiscussable issues

So that

Results:

Shorter implementation times

Increased commitment

Higher-quality decisions

Increased learning

Improved working relationships

Greater personal satisfaction and well-being

Figure 7.1 Criteria of a Culture of Shared Responsibility of Learning

Step 2: Adhere to protocols

Protocols are means for structuring conversations that relate to sense making, problem-solving, and giving and receiving feedback while anchoring the exchange in psychological safety. A number of protocols have been discussed throughout this book and have a place in teacher discourse and decision-making. Table 7.2 illustrates recommended protocols for particular teacher work.

Sense Making: Reviewing data, learning a new concept, and/or exploring a new practice	**Problem-Solving:** Working to solve a problem and make a decision	**Feedback:** Giving and receiving information on a person's performance through asking questions or seeking/giving advice
Harkness protocol In2out Final Word protocol SWOT protocol	What? So What? Now What?	Critical Friends Tuning protocol Learning Dilemma

Table 7.2 Protocols for Enhancing Effective Communication

Step 3: Engage in routine process and outcome checks

Maintaining an inquisitive stance regarding outcome and process can support teams in doing the right work. *Outcome* accountability centers people and teams on ensuring they are measuring their progress toward overall results. *Process* accountability centers people and teams on their progress along the way and how effective their daily decisions are on sticking with habits or changing/deviating habits. Over time, these layers of accountability help people get better at, change, or eliminate a habit.

Outcome-Based Questions

What are we going after? What are the goals of student learning? What are the goals of my own learning? How will I know if I'm successful?

Process-Based Questions

How will I know if my decision-making for my actions was appropriate? How will I check in and adjust over time? How will we work together to engage in this process collectively?

Habit 14: **Sprint** *by adhering to a rapid improvement process*

The recommendation here is to engage in a rapid inspection process of our impact on student learning by following a simple "learning sprint" process. This process is anchored to a set of questions, tenets, and specific actionable steps.

Questions that guide this work include:

✳ To what extent did we move toward one year's growth in one year's time across all levels of learning?

✳ To what extent did we maintain a level of shared power and responsibility with students?

✳ To what extent are our students developing the knowledge and skills to effectively engage independently and interdependently in their learning?

✳ To what extent did we introduce, define, sustain, or improve on our habits?

Adopted from Simon Breakspear and Bronwyn Ryrie Jones (2021), this process is anchored on the following key tenets:

✳ "Stay small, stay focused" – Pick a specific outcome to focus on for learning; pick a specific habit to put in place, eliminate, refine, or deviate from; and pick a select few students to monitor their progress over time.

✳ "Bias to action" – Focus the sprint on actionable habits that are likely to make an impact. Focus on only a few students and one specific habit. Make it doable, not exhausting. Remember—action without inspection will simply repeat the same actions. Deepening and improving are key and why the habits here are critical.

✳ "Go slow to go fast" – Conduct the same sprint a few times through. There are often times when the results from our actions take time. Lag time is going to be significant in the impact of our habits on students. This is especially true when students are engaging in deep and transfer learning.

✳ "Stay connected" – Work with others by sharing your results, discussing the interpretations from your results, and planning next steps.

Success Criteria: *Adhere to a rapid improvement process*

A process for rapid inspection can take many shapes and go by many names. Action research, inquiry cycles, and so forth are all going after reflection and improvement. Learning sprints are our preferred method because of their emphasis on small, measurable changes in a manageable amount of time. The process is outlined below. Learning sprints are anchored to five steps that enable them to take place quickly and effectively.

1. **Define** – Teachers define the specific outcomes they want to improve or innovate on. (See the online Appendix for a list of core outcomes for student learning.)

2. **Understand** – Develop a hypothesis for the reasons why this is an important focus area for the teachers to engage in.

3. **Plan** – Plan for the habit that you will use to improve outcomes. Remember success here relies on an action that is so simple it can be made habitual. Consider introducing, eliminating, refining, or deviating from a habit in the classroom.

4. **Sprint** – Implement the habit and, if possible, receive support from others in implementation. This requires teachers to focus on one habit; teach to a few students and allow a few weeks to inspect their impact in the moment and over time.

5. **Review and Reset** – Meet with others and review the results of their actions on student learning. This is where teachers determine key learning from the experience and potential next steps.

Learning Sprint Template
Team Members: _____ Date: _____
Define *What outcomes do we want to improve, and for which learners?* ***Notes:***
Understand ~ *Why is this a focus for me/us?* ~ *What's in the way of enhancing or improving this outcome currently?* ***Notes:***
Identify a Habit ~ *How can we better engage in a routine practice to support student engagement and progression?* ~ *What actionable habit will I put in place, eliminate, refine, or deviate from in order to improve student learning?* ~ *Where will I place this habit with what I'm already doing?* ***Notes:***

Learning Sprint Template
Sprint   ~ How will we know whether students are making progress?   ~ How many students will I monitor the impact of this habit on?   ~ How will I implement the habit? Who will support me in implementing this habit?   **Notes:**
Review and Reset   ~ What did we learn?   ~ What should we do next?   **Notes:**

Table 7.3 Learning Sprint Template

Habit 15: **Choose action** *by implementing a personalized plan for improving habits*

The same delusions of overconfidence that tempt competitors around a poker table can challenge teachers when we look squarely at our evidence. Rapid impact cycles have a way of shaping new stories for us. Were we certain our new strategy would work, only to find that it didn't change outcomes for students? Did we realize something new that was only a peripheral result of our focus? Did we learn something unexpected about our students themselves? Reviewing the results of the impact cycle will help to determine whether we need to stick to, modify, change from, or eliminate habits to enhance student outcomes. From our learning-sprint work, we may have found evidence that inspires us to start anew, igniting a whole new habit. We may find that we need to engage in longer-term refinement and practice. We may find that it is time to deviate and find new approaches to an old habit that has become all too familiar and is lagging in the impact we desire.

Success Criteria: *Implement a personalized plan for improving habits*

The activity in Table 7.4 can help plan for developing a new habit (or habits) for improving/refining your craft to impact student learning.

What action habit will I develop/refine/change/eliminate . . .
What should be an expected result of this habit related to student learning . . .
How will I develop this habit . . .
Who will support me in this habit development . . .
How will I improve . . .
Table 7.4 Individual Habit Development Action Plan

Encouraging Deliberate Deviations in Our Practices

The habits and criteria in this book are suggestions to improve student learning. They are hypotheses. Based on research and practice, they seem roughly right, but they likely are not going to work everywhere. Before we end this chapter, we have included a few additional strategies on promoting and supporting deliberate deviations in our habits. Students, teacher personalities, classroom culture, and even the time of year or the time of day create unique contexts that make situations unique. To craft our habits in a way that works for the real learning in our own classrooms, deviations are often necessary.

Adam Grant has expanded on this idea of experimenting and diverging as we put new ideas (and habits) to the test. In *Think Again*, he writes, "As Jeff Bezos explained . . . in an annual shareholder letter, instead of demanding convincing results, experiments start with asking people to make bets. 'Look, I know we disagree on this but will you gamble with me on it?' The goal in a learning culture is to welcome these kinds of experiments, to make rethinking so familiar that it becomes routine" (Grant, 2021, p. 219). Inasmuch, deviating from the norm may be the habit most worth cultivating.

Questions that can prime us for deliberate deviations include the following:

❊ How do we shift from best practices to better practices? Where are the nuances and complexities in my own context that I should look to change?

❊ Where is the "space between" in our work? What questions are we not asking that may lead us to new innovations in our practices and new learning for our students?

❊ How do we shift from models to sketches? How do we give ourselves permission to change our minds and actions over time?

When it comes to deviating, maybe we need to think with an identity different from that of "teacher." If that identity seems too confining, try thinking like someone who deviates as a matter of practice—if only for the sake of approaching learning with new eyes. Two examples are listed below:

1. Approach learning as an explorer: Seek nuance, not generalities. There is a high likelihood that you will find a habit you are using is not reaching every child, or illustrates that while it works for improving learning, students' emotional engagement declines. Instead of scrapping our habits altogether or staying strong despite the evidence, there is an opportunity to see whether a subtle shift could be included. In Chapter 3, we discussed how one teacher changed his driving question to focus on the present tense rather than the past to motivate students. He kept the habit of using inquiry to drive instruction but made a subtle shift. These subtle shifts are exactly what should be attempted, documented, and discussed to improve our work.

Find subtle differences. Ask specific questions about the professional learning you are about to undertake, such as the following:

✳ What nuances can I find that will push my thinking and/or my practice?

✳ What evidence would refine my current thinking or prove my current thinking wrong?

✳ What is unknown? What are people still trying to figure out? Where can I add value to this practice?

2. Approach learning as a photographer: Look through the eyes of students. Take a snapshot of student evidence of success. Mark down the degree to which your students are actually demonstrating what you want them to learn. There's a good chance that the learning is not an either-or proposition. That is, your students are likely all learning something. Where are they succeeding? Who is succeeding? Why are they succeeding? This will be useful in your determination of next steps in your own learning.

The status quo is a lofty opponent. It may be that we are slow to change because of our bias toward what's already being done. Actions we established early in our teaching career may change very little, regardless of new information. As discussed in the past several chapters, we may engage in "placebo action," or motion habits, but when we get to the moment of action in our classrooms, we tend to fall back on our "best practices." The challenge with best practices is that they maintain a status quo and prohibit our ability to search for even better practices. Moreover, it asks us to ignore the nuances and complexities that color our lived experience with students.

As we discover new nuances in our impact, we will make subtle adjustments. Our hope is that the readers of this book—and, better yet, the implementers of this work—challenge our thinking and our approach. This is how we build stronger and more interesting teaching strategies, expand our impact, develop and/or rekindle our own motivation, and improve student learning and well-being.

Calibrating Deliberate Practice and Deliberate Deviations as a Team

Table 7.5 walks through scenarios that teachers often find themselves in when determining next steps with their habits. When teachers start a new habit, they are in the ignition phase. They likely need support in implementation through modeling or in situ coaching. As teachers develop proficiency, they engage in deliberate practice. Deliberate practice is best defined as following a script repeatedly to develop proficiency. Teachers may be found concentrating on following the exact rules of a strategy with fidelity to get the strategy done right.

At times, there is an opportunity to deliberately deviate from the intended habit. If deliberate practice entails sticking to the script over and over so it begins to feel natural, deliberate deviation is thoughtfully going off script. As teachers, we improvise all the time; to deliberately deviate is to make changes to the strategy while still moving toward the outcome the strategy was built for. Here teachers are focused more on making subtle or significant changes to the strategy as a means for a greater level of impact on student learning. Deliberate deviation sounds like "I tried it this way, and it worked even better." The more this becomes encouraged, even systematic, the greater the wealth of different strategies and contemporary learning will build across teacher teams.

To sustain this work, teams need to monitor their overall process of igniting new habits, deliberate practice, and deliberate deviation. Table 7.5 features questions teachers may review quarterly with colleagues to determine if there is a need to recalibrate or stick with their current process of learning.

Habit Development Process Phase	Questions	Description
Ignition	Are we beginning a new habit? Are we eliminating a habit?	Start a new habit that has a tendency to develop a high impact on students. *Example: Give three target students in-the-moment feedback related to success criteria, four times per week.*
Deliberate practice	Are we refining the development of a habit? Are we working on sustaining this habit by embedding it with other habits? Am I doing this the right way?	Deliberately practice that new habit while inspecting our impact on that strategy in the classroom. *Example: To refine the habit of immediate feedback for target students, I will ensure there is enough time for independent practice so that I get to the students before we transition.*
Deliberate deviation	After investigating the impact of the habit on student learning, explore changes in action-based habits that may have a greater impact on student learning and push innovation. Are there other ways to meet our outcomes?	We should continue to investigate our approaches to igniting, practicing, and deviating from core habits that improve student learning. *Example: I need to deviate from giving corrective feedback for two of the three target students; I have a hunch open-ended process questions would be better feedback.*

Habit Development Process Phase	Questions	Description
Deliberate monitoring of motion and action habits	Are we using a wealth of evidence that gives us a clear understanding of student progress, proficiency, and perception? Do we have a balance of starting, stopping, continuing, or modifying/innovating?	Teams are monitoring their progress in taking action to improve learning and how to continue to grow in their teaching and learning. *Example: The feedback habit helped my students make fewer errors a month ago. Somehow I got out of practice, though, and need to reengage.*

Table 7.5 Core Process for Improving Student Learning and Habit Formation

Just as building habits of physical exercise requires repetition, schedule reconfiguration, and a healthy dose of self-compassion, implementing habits in the classroom requires support. To begin, sustain, eliminate, or innovate habits, certain criteria can make developing the habit more doable. The following criteria have been derived from the work of James Clear's (2018) *Atomic Habits*; they are meant to support new habits that improve teaching and learning. In addition, Table 7.6 illustrates suggested strategies for implementing and sustaining habits.

Habit Success Criteria	Description
Consistency versus intensity	Habits should occur daily and should be practical to the extent that the habit could be sustained forever. As such, habits should not be based on number of projects or end dates (e.g., I will have completed three co-construction activities by March). Habits should be based on daily practices that are manageable and sustainable.

Habit Success Criteria	Description
Stacking versus isolating	Layering is the concept of adding a new habit to one we are already implementing. This is more impactful than trying to conduct a new habit by itself.
Collaborative versus individual	Habits stick better when we do them with others. We need accountability, support, and a role in supporting others in their work.
Leveraging and integrating versus succession	Habits tend to have a higher impact when we integrate new habits together as opposed to implementing one and then attempting another later. While we don't want to overwhelm ourselves if we are attempting more than one strategy, finding a way to implement them at the same time may be beneficial.

Table 7.6 Habit Efficacy Success Criteria

Table 7.7 provides suggested strategies to support habit development.

Habit Implementation Strategies	Description
Stacking	Before I do . . . After I do . . . In between _____ and _____, I will . . .
Set Plays	~ Set a time during a lesson that will focus specifically on one habit. ~ Have an observer there to witness the habit and provide you with praise for giving it a go. ~ Over time, seek feedback and refine the habit.
In Situ	~ Witness a model and then immediately implement. ~ Debrief process.

Habit Implementation Strategies	Description
Interleaving	~ Incorporate a wide range of learning intentions and outcomes. ~ Incorporate a wide variety of instructional and feedback strategies.
Fade In	~ How do I make this habit super easy for me? ~ How can I make it obvious to me and others?
Integrating or Leveraging	~ Combine deep-to-transfer strategies with anchor strategies (e.g., clarity strategy with a deep-learning protocol)

Table 7.7 Habit Implementation Strategies

 Conclusion

The gap between what we know and what we don't know need not be untraversable. Within the safe parameters of a sound mind and supportive colleagues, any evidence—whether it be of robust learning or a lack thereof—can be a lever for refining habits until they work for the learners in the room. Measuring and responding to our impact individually, with students and with colleagues, is critical to determining our impact and deciding on what next steps we should take in our teaching and learning.

We quoted Maria Konnikova's statement at the beginning of this chapter: "The more you learn, the harder it gets." It's not because a craft gets more difficult for the sake of getting stubborn. It's that the more we understand, the more we find actions to refine or questions to pursue. The learning is never over. But the more you learn, the better it gets.

❓ Review Questions

❋ What are key steps you can take with colleagues to "make discourse deliberate"?

❋ What are key steps you can follow to take action on one of the habits in this book?

❋ How do you currently measure your progress toward outcomes? How do you measure your success in adhering to a habit or set of habits?

❋ How do you ensure deliberate deviation in your practices?

❋ How would you incorporate learning sprints into your practice? How would you develop a collaborative approach to this work?

🏃 Next Steps

❋ Identify a key habit to initiative or deviate from to impact student learning.

❋ Attempt a learning sprint and share your key learning with colleagues.

❋ Incorporate norms into your collaborative work with colleagues.

SUMMARY

> " You do not rise to the level of your goals. You fall to the level of your systems. Your goal is your desired outcome. Your system is the collection of daily habits that will get you there. This year, spend less time focusing on outcomes and more time focusing on the habits that precede the results.
>
> —James Clear

The primacy of surface teaching and learning is linked to our systems of habit as teachers. Attempts at changing these systems have been based largely on changing belief systems, building motion-based habits, and setting goals. As we read through-out the book, motion and actions both require effort. Action habits, however, pro-vide results. The work of teachers is to employ action habits that are linked to deep-to-transfer learning and habits that we engage in on a daily basis. By changing our habits in this direction, we will ensure students develop the knowledge and skills to take responsibility over their own learning, as well as work in an interdependent space with others to solve rich, authentic problems.

We need to stay small and stay focused on a few action habits that are doable for us and our students. We do not need to worry about spending time on building a set number of projects or worrying about the overall design and quantity of projects for a year. Quotas such as these place deep and transfer learning as a side act and situate project-based learning as a methodology built of products rather than the process of learning and problem-solving.

The environment in which teachers operate can pose obstacles. Classrooms are like habitats; the living beings within utilize a system of habits to survive and thrive. Classrooms have been designed to privilege surface knowledge and limit deep-to-transfer teaching and learning. Change must occur by staying small and staying focused on a few habits that enable teachers to rise above the preconditions that have been set for them and their students.

This book laid out a number of habits that, when put together, create steps that align to create four phases of rigorous problem- and project-based learning. Our hope is that you as a practitioner home in on one or two habits and build a level of proficiency there, and then scale over time to build more habits. Success begets success. Let's bring deep and transfer to be not only ignited in our classrooms but sustained for generations to come. Here is to the turtle race! We're right there with you, going slow to go fast.

REFERENCES

Alter, A. L., Oppenheimer, D. M., Epley, N., & Eyre, R. N. (2007). Overcoming intuition: Metacognitive difficulty activates analytic reasoning. *Journal of Experimental Psychology: General, 136*(4), 569–576.

Argyris, C. and Schön, D. (1978), *Organizational learning: a theory of action perspective.* New York: McGraw-Hill.

Biggs, J. B., & Collis, K. F. (1982). *Evaluating the quality of learning—the SOLO Taxonomy* (1st ed.). Academic Press.

Billings, E., & Mueller, P. (n.d.). *Quality student interactions: Why are they crucial to language learning and how can we support them?* Office of Bilingual Education and World Language. New York State Education Department. http://www.nysed.gov/common/nysed/files/programs/bilingual-ed/quality_student_interactions-2.pdf.

Breakspear, S., & Jones, B. R. (2021). *Teaching sprints: How overloaded educators can keep getting better.* Corwin.

Clarke, S. (2021). *Unlocking learning intentions and success criteria: Shifting from product to process across the disciplines.* Corwin.

Claxton G. (2019, April 9). Unfixing the growth mindset. *Claxton.* https://www.guyclaxton.net/post/unfixing-growth-mindset.

Claxton, G. (2021). *The future of teaching and the myths that hold it back.* Routledge.

Clear, J. (2018). *Atomic habits: An easy and proven way to build good habits and break bad ones.* Penguin Random House.

DaCosta, M. (1962). *The music man.* Warner Bros. Pictures.

Diemand-Yauman, C., Oppenheimer, D., & Vaughan, E. (2011). Fortune favors the bold (and the italicized): Effects of disfluency on educational outcomes. *Cognition, 118*(1), 111–115.

Deutscher, R. R., Holthuis, N.C., Maldonado, S. I., Pecheone, R. L., Schultz, S. E., Wei, R. C., & Lucas Education Research. (2021). Project-based learning leads to gains in science and other subjects in middle school and benefits all learners. Lucas Education Research.

Duke, N. K., Halvorsen, A. L., Strachan, S. L., Kim, J., & Konstantopoulos, S. (2021). Putting PBL to the test: The impact of project-based learning on second graders' social studies and literacy learning and motivation in low-SES school settings. *American Educational Research Journal*, 58(1), 160–200.

Epstein, D. (2019). *Range: Why generalists triumph in a specialized world.* Riverhead Books.

Ferlazzo, L. (2020, January 28). Author interview with Dr. Gholdy Muhammad: "Cultivating Genius." *EdWeek.* https://www.edweek.org/teaching-learning/opinion-author-interview-with-dr-gholdy-muhammad-cultivating-genius/2020/01

Freire, P. (2000). *Pedagogy of the oppressed* (30th anniversary ed.). Continuum.

Gawande, A. (2013, July 22). Slow ideas. *The New Yorker.* https//www.newyorker.com/magazine/2013/07/29/slow-ideas.

Gonzalez, J. (2013, October 24). *Students sitting around too much? Try chat stations.* https://www.cultofpedagogy.com/chat-stations.

Grant, A. (2021). *Think again: The power of knowing what you don't know.* Viking.

Haberman, M. (1991). The pedagogy of poverty versus good teaching. *Phi Delta Kappan,* 73(4), 290–294.

Hammond, Z. (2015). *Culturally responsive teaching and the brain: Promoting authentic engagement and rigor among culturally and linguistically diverse students.* Corwin.

Hattie, J. (2009). *Visible learning: A synthesis of over 800 meta-analyses relating to achievement.* Routledge.

Hattie, J. (2012). *Visible learning for teachers: Maximizing impact on learning.* Routledge.

Hattie, J. (2021a, March 22). *We need to get better at learning transfer.* World Education Summit. https://www.tes.com/magazine/archived/john-hattie-we-need-get-better-learning-transfer.

Hattie, J. (2021b). Visible Learning Metax. https://www.visiblelearningmetax.com/Influences.

Hattie, J., & Donoghue, G. M. (2016). Learning strategies: A synthesis and conceptual model. *Science of Learning, 1*(16013). https://thinkplusjourney.info/images/Hattie_and_Donoghue_-_Learning_strategies._A_synthesis_and_conceptual_model.pdf.

Hattie, J. & Timperley, H. (2007). The power of feedback. *Review of Educational Research, 77*(1), 81–112.

Hook, P. (2022, in press). *SOLO Taxonomy and hexagonal thinking: Using hexagons to think critically, creatively and collaboratively*. Essential Resources.

Hook, P. (n.d.). HookED SOLO Hexagon Generator. https://pamhook.com/solo-apps/hexagon-generator/.

Johnson, S. (2011). *Where good ideas come from: The natural history of innovation*. Riverhead Books.

Kirschner, P. A., Sweller, J., & Clark, R. E. (2006). Why minimal guidance during instruction does not work: An analysis of the failure of constructivist, discovery, problem-based, experiential, and inquiry-based teaching. *Educational Psychologist, 2*(2), 75–86.

Knight, J. (2022). *The definitive guide to instructional coaching: Seven factors for success*. Association for Supervision and Curriculum Development.

Konnikova, M. (2021). *The biggest bluff: How I learned to pay attention, master myself, and win*. Penguin.

Krajcik, J., Schneider, B., Miller, E., Chen, I.-C., Bradford, L., Bartz, K., Baker, Q., Palinscar, A., Peek-Brown, D., & Codere, S. (2021). *Assessing the effect of ML-PBL on science learning* [Technical report]. https://mlpbl.open3d.science/sites/mlpbl/files/MLPBL-technical-report.pdf.

Lucas Education Research. (2021). The Evidence is clear: Rigorous project-based learning is an effective lever for student success. Lucas Education Research.

Maclean, N. (1992). *Young men and fire*. University of Chicago Press.

Mannion, J., & McAllister, K. (2020). *Fear is the mind killer: Teaching children how to learn*. John Catt Educational.

Marzano, R. J. (2009). *Formative assessment and standards-based grading*. Marzano Research Laboratory.

Marzano, R. J. (2017). *The new art and science of teaching* (rev. and expanded ed.). Solution Tree Press.

McDaniel, M. A., & Butler, A. C. (2011). A contextual framework for understanding when difficulties are desirable. In A. S. Benjamin (Ed.), *Successful remembering and successful forgetting: A festschrift in honor of Robert A. Bjork* (175–198). Psychology Press.

McDowell, M. (2017). *Rigorous PBL by Design: Three shifts for developing confident and competent learners.* Corwin.

McDowell, M. (2020). *Teaching for transfer: A guide for designing learning with real-world application.* Solution Tree Press.

McDowell, M. (2021a). *Rigorous PBL by Design foundations workbook.* Mimi and Todd Press.

McDowell, M. (2021b). *Rigorous PBL by Design deep dive workbook.* Mimi and Todd Press.

McDowell, M. (2021c). *Developing expert learners: A roadmap for growing confident and competent students.* Corwin.

McDowell, M. (2021d). *The busy teacher: Differentiation for every classroom.* First Educational Resources

McNamara, D. S., & Kintsch, W. (1996). Learning from texts: Effects of prior knowledge and text coherence. *Discourse Processes, 22*(3), 247–288.

McTighe, J. & Gareis, C. (2021, June 10). Assessing deeper learning after a year of change. *ASCD Express, 16*(19). www.ascd.org/ascdexpress.

McTighe, J., & Wiggins, G. (2013). *Essential questions: Opening doors to student understanding.* Association for Supervision and Curriculum Development.

Mehta, J. (2018, January 4). A pernicious myth: Basics before deeper learner. *Education Week.* https://www.edweek.org/teaching-learning/opinion-a-pernicious-myth-basics-before-deeper-learning/2018/01.

Miller, L. (2019). *Unit 7 pre-quiz* [Handout]. Silverado Middle School, Math I.

Moser, J. S., Schroder, H. S., Heeter, C., Moran, T. P., & Lee, Y.-H. (2011). Mind your errors: Evidence for a neural mechanism linking growth mind-set to adaptive posterror adjustments. *Psychological Science, 22*(12), 1484–1489.

Nuthall, G. (2007). *The hidden lives of learners.* NZCER Press.

Paul, A. M. (2021). *The extended mind: The power of thinking outside the brain.* Houghton Mifflin Harcourt.

Potash, B. (2020, September 11). *Hexagonal thinking. A colorful tool for discussion.* https://www.cultofpedagogy.com/hexagonal-thinking/.

Powell, J., & Menedian, S. (2016). The problem with othering: Towards inclusiveness and belonging. *Othering and Belonging, 1*(1), 14–39.

Prather, C. (2021, December 6). The code for student engagement. Association for Supervision and Curriculum Development. https://www.ascd.org/el/articles/the-code-for-student-engagement.

Reeves, D. (2011). *Finding your leadership focus: What matters most for student results.* Teachers College Press.

Robert Schwarz (2016) The Skilled Facilitator: A Comprehensive Resources for Consultants, Facilitators, Coaches, and Trainers (3rd Ed.) Jossey-Bass

Rothermel, R. C. (1993). *Mann Gulch fire: A race that couldn't be won.* GTR INT-299. Ogden, UT: U.S. Department of Agriculture, Forest Service, Intermountain Research Station. 10 p.

Saavedra, A. R., Liu, Y., Haderlein, S. K., Rapaport, A., Garland, M., Hoepfner, D., Morgan, K. L., & Hu, A. (2021). Knowledge in action efficacy study over two years. University of Southern California Center for Economic and Social Research.

Sloman, S., & Fernbach, P. (2017). *The knowledge illusion: Why we never think alone.* Riverhead Books.

Smith, S. M., Glenberg, A., & Bjork, R. A. (1978). Environmental context and human memory. *Memory & Cognition, 6*(4), 342–353. https://doi.org/10.3758/BF03197465

Sousa, D. (2017). *How the brain learns.* Corwin.

Terada, Y. (2021, February 21). New research makes a powerful case for PBL. *Edutopia.* https://www.edutopia.org/article/new-research-makes-powerful-case-pbl.

Wexler, N. (2019). *The knowledge gap: The hidden cause of America's broken education system—and how to fix it.* Avery.

Willingham, D. (2021). *Why don't students like school? A cognitive scientist answers questions about how the mind works and what it means for the classroom* (2nd ed.). Jossey-Bass.

Yue, C., Castel, A., & Bjork, R. (2013). When disfluency is—and is not—a desirable difficulty: The influence of typeface clarity on metacognitive judgments and memory. *Memory and Cognition* 41, 229–241.

INDEX

Rigorous PBL Design Habit	Success Criteria
Habit 1: Make it clear	Create student-friendly learning intentions and success criteria at surface, deep, and transfer levels of learning
Habit 2: See it everywhere	Generate multiple contexts and one or more driving questions
Habit 3: Plan for the right fit	Align tasks across surface, deep and transfer expectations Design entry events, curveballs, and sequels for transfer
Habit 4: Lock it in	Set tentative dates for workshops aligned to complexity levels

The Project Habit: **Making Rigorous PBL by Design Doable**

Rigorous PBL Habit	Success Criteria
PHASE 1	
Habit 5: Start with a challenge *Where are we going?*	Set your purpose with an entry event Get students clear on what they're learning and what success looks like
Habit 6: Name the gaps *Where are we now?*	Pre-assess and discuss the results with students
Habit 7: Look ahead *What's next?*	Create next steps based on knows/need-to-knows (K/NTKs) Hold to learning agreements and protocols
PHASE 2	
Habit 8: Build the foundation	Apply instructional and feedback strategies to support surface-level learning
PHASE 3	
Habit 9: Question everything, together	Intentionally share power through structured discussions Use deep-level instructional and peer-to-peer feedback strategies Incorporate formative assessments that promote reflection and action.
PHASE 4	
Habit 10: Return to transfer	Revisit the entry experience, driving questions, learning intentions, and success criteria to determine key K/NTKs Implement transfer-level workshops to apply learning in real-world contexts and address curveballs
Habit 11: Deliver on the challenge	Structure means for showcasing work and giving/receiving feedback Engage students in project sequels
Habit 12: Look in the mirror	Conduct reflective protocols on academic growth Meet cultural expectations Address the DQ

Rigorous PBL Inspection Habit	Success Criteria
Habit 13: Make discourse deliberate	Agree to shared values and behaviors for shared work. Follow through on them.
Habit 14: Sprint	Adhere to a rapid improvement process
Habit 15: Choose action	Implement a personalized plan for improving habits

THE **CORE**
COLLABORATIVE

Professional Learning...
Personalized.

Partner with The Core Collaborative to co-design strengths-based, sustainable professional learning for measurable impact.

We believe that under the roof of every school is the talent and passion to make a difference for every learner. Together, we will unlock that potential by embracing the strengths, creativity, and curiosity of each member of your learning community.

Contact a learning expert at The Core Collaborative to discuss how we can support your goals.

619-432- CORE (2673)
thecorecollaborative.com/contact

Our EmpowerEd Learner Pathways of professional learning cover a wide range of topics:

PROFESSIONAL LEARNING
COMMUNITIES
Empower teacher teams to cultivate collaborative expertise and advance learner agency.

LEARNER-CENTERED
LEADERSHIP
Advance and nurture the conditions to craft, support, and sustain learner-centered systems.

LEARNER-CENTERED
ASSESSMENT
Design and execute a systemic, balanced, and learner-centered assessment framework.

BELONGING FOR
EQUITY
Advance learner agency through cultivating a culture of trust, belonging, healing, and efficacy.

LEARNER-CENTERED
INSTRUCTION
Cultivate a culture of inquiry, collaboration and discussion in your system.

LEARNER-CENTERED
CURRICULUM
Develop an equitable, viable, and coherent curriculum for absolutely every learner.

CONNECTED
CLIMATE
Cultivate a climate of connection that is trauma aware, trauma informed, and resiliency focused.